Internet
Piracy

CONTROVERSY!

Internet
Piracy

Gail Blasser Riley

Marshall Cavendish
Benchmark
New York

Other Marshall Cavendish Offices:
Marshall Cavendish International (Asia) Private Limited, 1 New Industrial Road,
Singapore 536196 • Marshall Cavendish International (Thailand) Co Ltd. 253 Asoke, 12th Flr,
Sukhumvit 21 Road, Klongtoey Nua, Wattana, Bangkok 10110, Thailand •
Marshall Cavendish (Malaysia) Sdn Bhd, Times Subang, Lot 46, Subang Hi-Tech Industrial Park,
Batu Tiga, 40000 Shah Alam, Selangor Darul Ehsan, Malaysia

Marshall Cavendish is a trademark of Times Publishing Limited
All websites were available and accurate when this book was sent to press.

Library of Congress Cataloging-in-Publication Data
Riley, Gail Blasser. • Internet piracy / • p. cm. — (Controversy!)
Includes bibliographical references and index.
ISBN 978-0-7614-4902-7
1. Piracy (Copyright)—United States. 2. Peer-to-peer architecture (Computer networks)—
Law and legislation—United States. 3. Copyright and electronic data processing—United States.
4. Sound recordings—Pirated editions—United States. 5. Piracy (Copyright)
6. Peer-to-peer architecture (Computer networks)—Law and legislation.
7. Copyright and electronic data processing. 8. Sound recordings—Pirated editions
I. Title. • KF3080.R55 2011 • 346.7304'82—dc22 • 2009050574

Publisher: Michelle Bisson • Art Director: Anahid Hamparian
Series Designer: Alicia Mikles • Photo research by Lindsay Aveilhe

The photographs in this book are used by permission and through the courtesy of:
Cover: Newscom; David McNew/Getty Images: 4; Nina Leen/Time Life Pictures/Getty Images:
8; Fotosearch: 13; Dave Benett/Getty Images: 16; Piko Press/Splash News and Pictures/Newscom:
22; George DeSota/Newsmakers/Getty Images: 26; AP Photo/Adam Nadel: 31; Reuters: 33;
Ron Edmonds/AP Photo: 41; Richard Sennott/Minneapolis Star Tribune/MCT/Newscom: 46;
Yuri Gripas/Reuters: 49; Eric Risberg/AP Photo: 53; Fredrick Persson/AFP/Getty Images: 58;
Olivier Morin/AFP/Getty Images: 64; Imaginechina/AP Images: 66; Ian Waldie/Getty Images: 73;
Steve Forrest/The New York Times/Redux: 75; Jim Wilson/The New York Times/Redux: 78.

Printed in Malaysia (T)
135642

Contents

Most people are so familiar with the text shown at the start of each DVD they play at home that they don't even think about what it means.

Introduction

THE PROTECTION OF CREATIVE PROPERTY HAS LONG been part of our legal system. The first U.S. copyright was issued in 1790, and copyright law today still protects creative work. As technology has evolved, so has the legal domain, expanding to include protection of intellectual property. People come into contact with intellectual property every day—through books, articles, songs, poems, movies, television shows, plays, software, inventions, and symbols.

As the Internet has become a common thread through our lives, it has provided a nurturing environment for viewing and sharing creative work. Over the course of a single day, a person might use software for work or play, download songs or listen to music and watch movies in real time, and exchange files with friends. All of these activities can be perfectly legal. They can also be acts of Internet piracy.

Prior to the general use of the Internet, if people wanted to share a song or a book, they exchanged the actual item. It was not feasible or easy to make multiple copies of musical recordings, books, and films.

When tape recorders were invented, people could more easily create copies of music and films, but mass distribution was still quite difficult until people began to use the Internet regularly in the 1990s. The speed of transmitting files electronically seemed startlingly fast in comparison. The easy production of digital files made it even faster and simpler.

Walking through a discount store, a consumer probably would not consider it legal or acceptable, socially or morally—to fill a basket with items from the shelves and walk out the door without paying for them. It's more difficult for some people to think in the same way about illegally downloading and transmitting music and movie files. Indeed, some have argued that these files should be freely shared—without legal penalties. This book explores the legal and moral debates regarding rights relative to intellectual property. While it is clear that Internet piracy is illegal, some claim that there is no moral injustice in taking materials that are freely available online. In fact, some believe the Internet is only one cog in the wheel of a cultural revolution that will organically and appropriately result in availability of intellectual property to all who can access it. Others believe that the availability of art does not mean that people should be able to make it their own without paying for it.

Just as police would pursue a thief who dashed out of a store without paying for items, it is reasonable to expect that law enforcement officers will pursue people who steal files via the Internet—if the files' content is protected by copyright.

As the years have passed, law enforcement agencies have diligently and creatively pursued both businesses and individuals engaging in Internet piracy, resulting in penalties such as prison time, probation, and fines. These businesses and individuals have also been defendants in civil cases and have had to pay substantial fines.

When a Coldplay album or a Star Wars film is leaked to the public over the Internet, the impact can be substantial. It is an impact that has given rise to philosophical discussions about freedom versus protection. This book examines both the philosophical and the pragmatic facets of the complex topic of Internet piracy.

1 From Analog to Digital: The Birth of File Sharing

1965: COUPLES FILLED THE DANCE FLOOR. A VINYL record hugged the turntable. The sharp needle settled into the first groove. As the turntable spun, strains of the Beatles made their way through the speakers. When the party wound down, one of the guests expressed an interest in playing the music at her own party the following week. She might borrow the vinyl record, or purchase a record of her own.

Fast-forward to 2000: Fingers hugged the keyboard and gripped the mouse. After a few clicks, strains of Eminem made their way through the sound-system speakers. Friends wanted to listen to Eminem, too, so, with a few more mouse clicks, the music was downloaded and on its way to friends around the world. A little wrinkle: The person clicking the mouse had broken criminal and civil laws. So had the website offering the Eminem song: P2P, peer-to-peer network, was born. It made downloads available in a fast and easy way. It provided a totally new and simple access to intellectual property. People were able to download songs without paying. A new controversy—and many lawsuits—would now make their way through cyberspace and land smack-dab in the middle of the public and legal consciousness.

In the early days of vinyl records, many people didn't even own record players. Stealing music was not much of a possibility.

It's clear that stealing music was barely possible during the days of vinyl records. As technology progressed, however, it became easier and easier to copy music—and other types of creative property. Courts and social commentators have been grappling with the issue for decades. New laws have been written to address this new type of theft. Law enforcement has struggled to develop technologies to catch those who download illegally—and those who provide free access to copyrighted works. And social commentators have come down on both sides of the moral argument. Some say that the intellectual property should not be taken without payment. Others say that it is art, freely available, and anyone who is able to access it should be allowed to have it without fear of legal repercussions.

People might wonder how someone can *steal* music or a movie performance or the words of a book. After all, they're not tangible items, like cars and clothing. Even so, creative works are still a type of property, and they are protected by law—just like physical and real property.

While most people clearly recognize items such as houses, cars, and clothing as property that can belong to someone, they might have more difficulty grasping the concept of intellectual property. Intellectual property exists as a result of creativity and is protected by copyright, patent, or trademark.

If someone stole your car—or your shoes—it would be clear the person had taken property that belonged to you. The same is true of intellectual property. If someone writes music or a book—or performs music—the creation belongs to them.

But not everyone sees it that way. Some say theft of a vehicle or other personal property is not at all the same as the theft of intellectual property. After all, they argue, when a car has been stolen, it is no longer in the possession of the property owner; it can no longer be used by the property owner. When intellectual property is copied for free, the owner still has it and can still profit from it. Many feel that musical artists, filmmakers, and others who have greatly profited from income generated by their intellectual property are being selfish. They have made huge sums of money, it is said, and they should not withhold their intellectual property from those who are able to access it for free. Others respond that theft of intellectual property is truly like theft of personal property. The property no longer holds the same value for the property owner, so, indeed, the property has been appropriated by another.

But the fact is that music, books, films, computer software, and other creative property are intellectual property. Such work is protected by copyright, trademark, or patent, and someone who steals it is guilty of theft.

Copyright, Patents, and Trademarks

Copyright is the legal right of an author, composer, publisher, or other creator of work to exclusively publish, distribute, print, or perform the work in public—or to grant the right, or license, to others to do so. Other types of intellectual property, inventions, for example, can be protected through patents. Still others, such as symbols, can be protected through a trademark—a legally registered name or symbol allowed to be applied only by the owner of the product. A trademark generally protects a patent.

Why Is Internet Piracy a Recent Phenomenon?

Computers existed during the 1940s, but they were clunky and huge—and were not available for use in people's homes and offices. Instead, they were located primarily on college campuses and in research facilities. And if there were any theft, because of the limited capabilities and numbers of computers, it would be relatively simple to detect a theft and track down the computer on which the crime was committed. It would be many decades before cyber-crimes, such as Internet piracy, would become widespread.

What Is Internet Piracy?

From the Motion Picture Association of America (MPAA): "Internet piracy is the downloading or distribution of unauthorized copies of intellectual property such as movies, television, music, games and software programs via the Internet."

From the Directors Guild of America (DGA): "Broadly defined, piracy is simply a genre of theft—the taking of someone else's property or goods without securing permission or paying a fee. As it relates to movies and television shows—forms of intellectual property (IP)—piracy is the unauthorized use, copying or distribution of copyrighted content."

From the Business Software Alliance (BSA): "Software piracy is the unauthorized copying or distribution of copyrighted software."

From the World Intellectual Property Organization (WIPO): "Intellectual property . . . refers to creations of the mind: inventions, literary and artistic works, and symbols, names, images, and designs used in commerce.

All the formal definitions boil down to a single, overarching principle. It is illegal to take property that belongs to another person, regardless of how it is taken or whether it is physical or intellectual property.

After the invention of audiotape recorders and videotape recorders (VTRs) and videocassette recorders (VCRs), people were able to create copies of music and films. They sometimes made these copies from existing originals, but they also made the recordings while attending live concerts or movie showings. Of course, the quality of these illegal recordings wasn't stellar, but they were still sold. In the early days, this theft was not Internet piracy, as no Internet existed.

Once the Internet became easily accessible, however, people could make these films in theaters or at concerts—and they could then create additional copies and offer them as downloads or as tapes or CDs through a variety of sources, including online auctions. The term coined for digitized copyrighted work transmitted over the Internet is "warez."

How Is Internet Piracy Committed?

There are a variety of ways to commit Internet piracy. Some of the most common include illegal use of P2P networks, page jacking, illegal use of cyber lockers, Internet theft of trade secrets, and illegal use of streaming video.

Page Jacking

Page jacking happens when people take content from a website without permission. Page-jacking revenue usually occurs after a substantial amount of content has been stolen from one website and posted to another. Then, when people use Internet search engines to look for keywords, the sites with the pirated content also come up as "hits."

Some take others' content for the purpose of selling it as hard copy. They print out the pages and sell the printed version. Some download the content and display it on a website; they may sell ads and obtain revenue when traffic is driven to the site and links on the site are clicked. Others are simply trying to drive traffic to a site totally unrelated to the content, such as a site that sells pornography. Often, once a user has clicked on the link to a site through a search-engine hit, the user is caught in a trap, unable to exit the site. The ability to click forward or backward is disabled. The use can escape only through the "history" arrow or by closing—and restarting—the browser.

As technology advances, search engines are better able to isolate page-jacker sites and stop them from appearing in search-result lists. And law enforcement agencies are becoming increasingly able to track the activities of these sites and prosecute the pirates.

Illegal Transmission of Digital Files through Peer-to-Peer Networks (P2P)

A peer-to-peer network, often referred to as a P2P, is a computer network that allows users to share digital files by transmitting them to one another through uploads and downloads.

One of the most common ways to commit Internet piracy is through a P2P network.

Streaming Video

Streaming video is compressed video transmitted and viewed in real time. After the video has been watched, there is no copy of the video file left on the viewer's computer. TV shows and movies have been released legally and illegally through streaming video.

Cyber Lockers

Cyber lockers are also known as digital lockers. These are online storage sites that allow users to upload large files—the size of commercial films—and allow other users to download the films. Some sites bring in revenue by facilitating a fast download of the content.

Not all cyber lockers are illegal. Some are used for legitimate streaming-video purposes; however, it is believed that the vast majority are used for illegal downloads.

Internet Theft of Trade Secrets

Most companies use their computers to maintain items such as business plans, privately developed software, blueprints, private employee information (including Social Security numbers and work history), and customer lists. By hacking into company computers, pirates access this information and then sell and disseminate it to interested parties around the world.

Sometimes, those who are purchasing these items don't realize they are dealing with Internet pirates. For example, these pirates might offer software at greatly reduced rates, but purchasers might think they are simply being provided a discount, rather than participating in a crime.

Star Wars Fading Out of Sight?

George Lucas, the developer and one of the writers of the *Star Wars* films, appeared before Congress after Internet leaks of *Star Wars*. Lucas, described as "visibly shaken" during his testimony,

Film Piracy: The Phantom Menace

In 2000, Jason Everett Spatafore, also known as Disman, a twenty-five-year-old computer technician from Arizona, pleaded guilty in U.S. Federal Court to criminal copyright infringement (Internet film piracy). The plea agreement stated that Spatafore, during a period of less than two months, "willfully infringed a copyright by reproducing and distributing by electronic means copies of parts of the film *Star Wars Episode I: The Phantom Menace*." Spatafore did this by posting copies of portions of the movie on a variety of websites where others could download copies through the Internet—and he encouraged others to do so. He said he had downloaded the film from an unauthorized fan site. He posted it on sites that paid him a small sum each time someone visited one of the sites—and one report stated that he earned only about $40 for doing so.

Spatafore noted that the Internet service provider kept removing the film. He said he'd thought this was because the file was too large, so he continued to post, breaking the file into smaller files. Reports state that Spatafore removed the film when an acquaintance told him he might be infringing copyright. Spatafore was sentenced to probation and a fine.

Internet movie piracy can mean the loss of big bucks for those who create the movies that are stolen and distributed illegally. One of those moviemakers is George Lucas *(left)*, pictured here at the Red Bull Star Wars Grand Prix Party in Monte Carlo, Monaco, around the time of the thefts. Some argue that Lucas was not truly injured by the thefts.

referenced the revenue lost as a result of leaks through the Internet. He identified such a substantial impact that he stated there might never be another film like the *Star Wars* saga.

Viewpoints differ regarding this pirating. Some argued that Lucas had already earned vast sums of money and was not truly injured. Others argued that the loss of revenue injured not just Lucas, but the plethora of people involved in the filmmaking and distribution process—from Lucas himself to movie theater cashiers.

Internet Theft of Digital Music and Video Files

Technology marched on and away from the earliest computers, as well as from the practice of analog recording, such as recording on vinyl records and videotape. By 1999, a new era was on the horizon. With the advent of MP3 music files, Napster was born.

MP3 music files were a new phenomenon. They were compressed encoded wave files, which meant that they greatly reduced the amount of data necessary to create a sound substantially the same as the original. The sound quality was excellent; however, the MP3s were a different medium than audio compact discs (CDs) and could hold more music. The new format made it possible for people to go online to search Napster, locate a song on another user's hard drive, and immediately download the song to a computer—without spending a dime. The song could be transferred to an MP3 player through use of a USB port. Then the user owned a copy of the song. Musical artists did not receive compensation for the downloads of their songs. The record labels were likewise deprived, and this loss of revenue had an impact on the thousands of people involved in producing the music.

The law had been set up so that those who owned the music held the copyright. Even today, the law stipulates that royalties—specified sums of money—are to be paid to musical artists and others responsible for production of the music each time the music is sold or distributed. If such compensation does not occur, the person pirating the intellectual property has violated the law and can be pursued for criminal and civil penalties. Napster had effectively cut off the rights of the artists and others involved in the music production to gain the money they were owed based on the copyright of the material.

Without laws to cover intellectual property rights, anyone—anywhere—could simply take the music, performance, script, book, art, or other intellectual property of others: in other words, it was "piracy." On the high seas, pirates steal from people on ships. And often, little can be done immediately to stop Internet pirates. It is difficult to trace the property and convict the wrongdoers in court.

And so it was with the emergence of Napster, considered by many to be the watershed of Internet piracy. Napster grew to 70 million subscribers—and many people saw nothing wrong with file sharing. Teens commented on the ease of obtaining the music, the pleasure of downloading it for free, and the feeling that convenience outweighed any ethical considerations. One college student said, "A lot of kids think, 'Why bother paying $18 for a CD when you only like one or two cuts. . . . You might be able to get a full CD of music you like from somebody who downloads it.'"

By 2004, the recording industry estimated losses of as much as $4.2 billion throughout the world from illegal downloads, resulting in a drop of 31 percent in album sales from the spring of 2000 to the spring of 2004.

Many musical artists were up in arms. And record label executives contacted legal teams to determine how they could stop the illegal flow of music. The situation was akin to shoppers entering a mall, searching for items they wanted, taking them off the shelves, and walking out without paying—only the theft was happening virtually, and it was occurring with intellectual property, which some folks still didn't see as property at all.

In 2000, Madonna's new song "Music" was leaked through

Napster before it was released to the public. It was scheduled to be released as a single and as the title song on her new album. Madonna's manager stated that the song was still a work in progress and was not scheduled to be released for a number of months. He said, "Ultimately those sites that offered a download of Madonna's music are violating her rights as an artist." Madonna's record label, Warner Brothers, made it clear that this downloading was considered a serious matter.

Also during 2000, Metallica and Dr. Dre filed claims against Napster for allowing people to use its servers to exchange copyrighted songs illegally. The battles against Napster were growing—and would soon erupt into a full-fledged legal war.

While this was happening with Napster, other types of Internet piracy were also occurring. Some websites were allowing the downloads or sales of films they did not own and had not obtained permission or a license to share. Other websites were selling and delivering unauthorized audiotapes and videotapes, as well as copied works of art, but the focus was definitely on Napster. Napster had become the fastest-growing system ever on the Internet. Users had to download the program, then create a screen name and search for titles. Searches were usually very fast, done in a matter of seconds or minutes, and then the user was able to download the song, making it available to play on an MP3 player or burn onto a CD.

Nineteen-year-old Shawn Fanning—a college dropout from Boston's Northeastern University and the creator and owner of Napster—had learned his craft from an uncle who owned a computer game company. While in college, Fanning had become a big participant in an online chat system. He discovered that college students were sending digital music files to one another, but were complaining that it was difficult to locate all the songs they wanted. Fanning and a couple of other students discussed possibilities for exchanging music files and ideas—and the development of Napster began.

Fanning named the software "Napster" because he'd garnered the nickname at an early age because of his bushy hair. Initially, Fanning had not set out to create a business; rather, it was just a way to share ideas and files. But there were expenses for Internet connections and hardware required to share the files; he created the business to fund the development and upkeep.

Many, including some intellectuals who believed in broad dissemination of art, praised Fanning for making music so easily available. They said the record companies and artists had made plenty of profit and shouldn't be greedy. They argued that Napster provided exposure, which was particularly valuable to newer artists. Such opinions were certainly not shared by all. Howie Klein, Reprise Records president, said, "The people who are on the board of directors and in the upper-level management of Napster all belong in prison." Many others shared Klein's opinion. Musicians including Madonna, Dr. Dre, Eminem, and Metallica ultimately filed lawsuits against Napster and Fanning. And the federal government pursued criminal charges.

Illegal Networks

Napster was not the only P2P providing free music downloads without a license. Others included Kazaa, LimeWire, Morpheus, and eDonkey. All of these companies' illegal operations were shut down as a result of lawsuits—or voluntarily by the companies themselves. After the lawsuits that had been already been filed—and the ongoing investigations—it was clear that such illegal operations were likely to be vigorously pursued with an eye toward civil and criminal sanctions, or penalties.

Why Does Internet Piracy Occur?

Some people don't know the law, though that is no legal excuse. Others know that what they are doing is illegal, but they disagree with the law, which, again, is no legal excuse. A survey in the *Wall*

Street Journal stated: "Consumers simply do not see bootlegged movies as illegal or morally wrong, perhaps because of the ease and anonymity of Internet downloads and the widespread consumer acceptance of obtaining fake movies."

Why Aren't These Operations Immediately Shut Down?

Initially, there is the problem of finding those who are behind the sites; however, an even larger problem exists when the pirates are located in countries other than the United States. Then the United States must track down people who are operating illegally outside the country; it is also necessary to procure the cooperation of foreign governments in the prosecution or extradition—the return of these people to the country where the crime is alleged to have been committed.

Once those believed to have committed the crimes are located, a legal case must be mounted against them. All of this requires extensive investigation and a great deal of time and money.

Argentinian singer Shakira believes that file sharing is a good thing: not a rip-off but a "democratization of music."

2 Viewpoint: Sharing and Promotion— or Theft?

A ROCKY CHASM DEVELOPED BETWEEN THOSE WHO thought of Shawn Fanning and his company, Napster, as benevolent purveyors of music and exposure for artists, and those who thought of Fanning and Napster as criminals who deserved to be punished.

Proponents of Napster and free file sharing espoused the benefits for culture and society: it allows art to be spread about freely, resulting in exposure and enjoyment for all people who are able to access the art. They liken the arguments against such free sharing to arguments against the printing press. The printing press disseminated information, and so does free sharing of art. Some said that Napster and other file sharing sites actually provided a benefit to musicians by exposing their music to a very wide audience, a phenomenon of particular value to new artists, whose careers could be kicked off in a big way. Those who proffered this view believed this new form of technology was to be honored, admired, and adapted to, rather than criticized. Some said the record companies opposed Napster and similar developing sites because they couldn't control the operations and content—and as huge record-company moguls, they were accustomed to having total control. Some who were in favor of file sharing believed the recording industry had skewed statistics to make it appear as though they were losing profits, when profits were not truly declining.

In 2009, musical artist Shakira stated that file sharing represented a "democratization of music." Speaking of music as a "gift," she said, "I like what's going on because I feel closer to the fans and the people who appreciate the music." Shakira believed the downloads would develop a wider fan base, people who were potential ticket-purchasers for her concerts, and she didn't see the file sharing as a bite out of profits.

Ed O'Brien of Radiohead expressed a similar opinion, stating he thought file sharing could lead to listeners' enjoying the music and buying the album or going to a concert as a result.

Nick Mason of Pink Floyd said, "The last thing we want to be doing is going to war with our fan base. File sharing means a new generation of fans for us."

The Electronic Frontier Foundation (EFF), which describes itself as "the leading civil liberties group defending your rights in the digital world," was—and remains—a strong advocate of file sharing, stating that copyright laws were in sore need of revision. The EFF offered a number of possible solutions, but did not believe criminal charges and civil sanctions were the appropriate way to address the issue. The EFF stated that laws designed to stop Internet piracy "chill[s] free expression and scientific research."

The First Amendment Center offers extensive information about the law and First Amendment rights on its website, which includes an article by first amendment specialist William K. Norton. In the article, Norton recognized the importance of copyright, but stated: "copyright litigation can also have the effect of stifling developing online technologies that have the potential to encourage future expression. In a sense, copyright gives its owner a monopoly on that expression." Norton said software could be viewed as expression—protected by the First Amendment. It was not only the expression of the content offered through the software, he commented, but the code used to create the software itself. As the Electronic Frontier Foundation and others had, Norton referenced a "chilling effect" of restrictions due to copyright on the software. He argued that software programmers might be forced to write totally new types of programs because they would fear lawsuits based on copyright infringement if they used coding mechanisms similar to those that had been used to create other programs. This could require programmers to "reinvent the wheel," he stated, or worse, it could stifle their moving forward to create new programs, as they could be ever fearful of a lawsuit.

Record stores near college campuses reported decreased CD sales, according to a 2001 article, "The Copyright Paradox," by lawyer Jonathan Band in the magazine *Brookings Review*. However, overall CD sales had risen by 8 percent since 2000, Band said. Analysts wondered if this might have been due to the easy accessibility of free online downloads. Perhaps college students were utilizing these downloads more than those outside college campuses, which would have explained the statistic.

At the beginning of the Napster fray, a number of musicians, including Grammy–winner Janis Ian, were quite vocal about their views. Ian published an article titled "The Internet Debacle" in *Performing Songwriter* magazine in 2002. Her position was that "free Internet downloads are good for the music industry and its artists." Ian said that the traffic to her own website had increased dramatically after Napster had allowed free downloads of her music. Within a month, Ian's article appeared on more than one thousand websites and was reprinted in newspapers. It was translated into nine languages. Ian was stunned at the response. After personally receiving thousands of comments, she published a follow-up article, titled "FALLOUT."

Ian's words and experience reflected the sentiments of these who did not object to online file sharing. Ian stated that when she

Shawn Fanning created Napster when he was in college. He remained a controversial figure in the music business and in legal circles for many years thereafter.

began research for the article, she hadn't yet formed an opinion as to whether downloading was wrong. The more she researched, though, the clearer her thoughts became.

Ian wrote that she did not believe downloading harmed the industry. And she thought consumers would still buy the music—even if they could download it for free. She likened the situation to consumers being able to access water for free, but still buying bottled water—because they had a reason for buying it. Ian cited her nephews' views, stating they preferred a specific CD to a download. Why? They wanted the art and the video available on the CD.

Ian's article detailed the record industry's desire to control the business. She cited an article published in April 2001 by Jon Hart and Jim Burger in the *Wall Street Journal*: "The record companies created Napster by leaving a void for Napster to fill." It could be said that their argument accused record companies of failing to meet the needs of the listening public by not making music readily and easily accessible.

One of the thousands of responses Ian received to her article came from Hilary Rosen. Rosen was president and CEO of the Recording Industry Association of America (RIAA). The RIAA is the trade group that represents the U.S. recording industry. Rosen sent material to Ian to explain the position of the RIAA, a position that was diametrically opposed to Ian's. RIAA held that Napster was violating copyright. It was disseminating music without an agreement—or license. As a result, musical artists lost copyright revenue. The record companies lost revenue. And the impact filtered down to the plethora of workers who had had a hand in producing the music. The RIAA filed—and won—a lawsuit against Napster in late 1999. By 2000, Napster stopped its operations.

Superstar Sir Elton John stated his comments about file sharing: "I am of the view that the unchecked proliferation of illegal downloading (even on a 'non-commercial' basis) will have a seriously detrimental effect on musicians, and particularly young musicians and those composers who are not performing artists."

Motion Picture Association of America (MPAA)

Another major player in the fight against Internet piracy is the Motion Picture Association of America (MPAA). By the mid–2000s, the MPAA stated that losses due to Internet piracy were in the billions. Some might have challenged this figure, but it was verified through MPAA record keeping. Like a number of other agencies, the MPAA has been a major player in the promotion of legislation designed to address Internet policy. It has also invested substantial sums to improve security, and it works to ferret out

Beyond Napster

Hilary Rosen left her post as president and CEO of the RIAA in 2003. By 2009—ten years after the birth of Napster—she had become a CNN commentator and managing partner of a public-relations and communications strategy firm. In an interview with *Billboard* magazine, she commented that Napster had changed the music industry by catalyzing the interaction of music fans and record companies in a way that was unprecedented. Where radio stations and record stations had been the primary customers for record companies prior to that point, music fans began to play a more vital—and more vocal—role in the process. Rosen explained that years earlier, she had privately concurred that record companies should come to a licensing agreement with Napster, but no one had done anything like this before. And even though Napster had agreed to go to a pay service, by that point, P2P had become much more widespread, and a solution had become much more complex. Even if the Napster issues had been resolved, illegal downloads were occurring through a variety of venues, so it was no longer a matter of stopping just Napster. The problem with illegal downloads had grown exponentially.

Sicko!

In 2007, filmmaker Michael Moore's film *Sicko* appeared on networks such as Pirate Bay and BitTorrent before it was released in theaters. Elizabeth Kaltman, spokesperson for the MPAA, said the motion picture industry worldwide lost more than $18.2 billion to piracy. Of this, slightly more than $7 million was lost as a result of *Internet* piracy. Kaltman referred to the issue as "a 'huge threat' to studios and filmmakers." But Moore provided free viewings of the film in order to make his point to a wide audience. His rights were not violated, but the MPAA objected. The desire to disseminate ideas about an issue does not give rise to the right to violate copyright, the MPAA said, despite the intentions of the artist. Moore may have been glad that his film reached a wider audience, but the MPAA was not.

Reports varied as to the amount of money lost. For example, the National Legal and Policy Center estimated the losses as approximately $2 billion, not $18.2 billion.

Internet pirates. It stresses its desire to move forward with new technologies that make movies available legally over the Internet.

Another assertion made by the MPAA is that organized crime has been linked to piracy. The MPAA states that criminals use the funds received as a result of pirating films for the purpose of supporting other illegal activities, such as the sale of narcotics and unlicensed guns.

The MPAA points out the importance of the movie industry to the United States, stating that it employs about 750,000 people. This figure includes those who work directly on the films, as well as those with a more indirect connection, such as electricians, drivers, carpenters, and food workers. And the MPAA identifies the benefit to local economies of a film shoot, citing a figure of approximately $200,000 contributed daily to local economies. Many businesses benefit from a film shoot. The MPAA's information helps to put a human face on the results of Internet piracy. While some might perceive the film industry as an impersonal monolith, the MPAA works to show that it is composed of many workers—and benefits those who work inside and outside the business. The MPAA's figures illustrate that piracy takes money out of the pockets of all sorts of folks, not just from the bank accounts of the superwealthy.

Business Software Alliance (BSA)

The Business Software Alliance (BSA) is another group that has been strongly committed to fighting Internet piracy. BSA identifies itself as the voice of the world's software industry and its hardware partners on a wide range of business and policy affairs. BSA has played an active role in working to stem the tide of Internet software piracy.

As BSA explains, purchasers of software are, in truth, buying a license to use the software, not the software itself. The license delineates how many times the software can be installed. If it is installed more times than allowed—or if it is copied—then soft-

Members of the entertainment industry, including *(right to left)* Jason Berman, chairman-elect of the International Federation of the Phonographic Industry; Strauss Zelnick, president and CEO of BMG Entertainment; Hilary Rosen, president and CEO of RIAA; and Ken Berry, president of EMI Recorded Music, listen to reporters' questions about the formation of a voluntary digital music security system.

ware piracy, a form of copyright infringement and theft, has been committed.

"Piracy over the Internet has increased both in breadth and sophistication in the last few years, and requires us to increase our efforts to combat the issue," said attorney Neil MacBride, BSA's vice president of antipiracy and general counsel. BSA shut down more than 13,800 illegal online auctions in 2007, addressing software products that had retail value of more than $13 million. During the first three months of 2008, BSA shut down almost three times as many auctions as it had during the same three months in 2007.

BSA implemented a $1-million reward program, which initially focused on piracy reported in the workplace; BSA extended the program in 2008 to include "the report of the sale of illegal software over the Internet," for example, on online auction sites. It's interesting to note that approximately half the people who reported such activity declined the reward. MacBride commented: "The existence of the rewards program drives strong awareness on behalf of the general public, but we find that many of our reports of software piracy come from those who recognize and respect the importance of intellectual property regarding business software."

The BSA reported prosecution of a man who infringed copyright by selling unlicensed copies of more than thirty-one software products. The man was sentenced in Mississippi to twenty-four months of imprisonment and three years of suspended supervisory release. He was also sentenced to pay approximately $46,000 in restitution. Proponents of free file sharing believe that such prosecutions should not be pursued at all, and many believe that imprisonment for this type of crime is not warranted.

The BSA conducted an undercover investigation of a woman who illegally sold copyright-protected software through e-mail offers. The case was referred to the United States Department of Justice, which prosecuted and sentenced the woman to six months in prison for copyright infringement.

On its website, BSA recounts additional stories of penalties to a number of Internet pirates. One was a young man who sold software illegally online. After committing this federal crime, he was sentenced to six years in prison. Additionally, he was directed to do fifty hours of community service. But that was not the total sentence. He was also directed to pay more than $4 million to the software publishers—due to loss of sales.

Another pirate, a retiree, sold copies of software through an online auction site. BSA ordered the software, had the item tested, and discovered it was counterfeit. Through a civil judgment, the court awarded $250,000.

A track star facing a world of opportunity dashed it all to make

The destruction of pirated materials has become a new growth industry. In Beirut, Lebanon, a bulldozer crushes hundreds of pirated CDs.

Copyright Police?

In 2007, telephone company and Internet service provider AT&T Inc., agreed to work with record and movie companies to seek out those who were uploading illegal films and music through services provided by AT&T. CEO and cofounder of Public Knowledge, attorney Gigi Sohn, warned that the likely result of AT&T's action would be alienated customers.

"We hope AT&T recognizes the difficulty of what it is trying to do," Sohn said. "By attempting to act as the copyright police, the company is going to make its customers angry, even in a market in which customers have little choice of providers for high-speed Internet service."

Claudia Jones of AT&T responded that AT&T did not intend to pursue average Internet users making downloads. Instead, she commented, AT&T and its media-industry partners would focus on locating those who profit by uploading illegally copied material for others to purchase. "Our goal is to balance the protection of copyrighted data with our customers' right to access and fair use of content on the Internet." In 2009, Jones confirmed the policy, but also stated that they would take no action without a court order.

some cash. He was a college sophomore who, with partners, sold illegal software online, stating that the items he offered were backup software. He was sentenced to three years in federal prison, with supervision for another three years after the prison time. He also received a fine in the amount of $10,000. Additionally, he was forced to give up his HDTV and computer equipment, as well as a very expensive luxury vehicle. In carrying out criminal prosecution, personal property and cash can sometimes be forfeited, seized by government authorities. According to the law, this property can then sometimes be sold, with the revenue going to the prosecuting entity, such as the federal government, or to the crime victims as restitution.

Free Riding

The group Public Knowledge identifies itself as "a Washington DC based public interest group working to defend your rights in the emerging digital culture." Alex Curtis is the director of policy and new media at Public Knowledge. During a radio program in 2007, Curtis discussed Internet piracy with MPAA president Fritz Attaway. Attaway referred to illegal file sharing as "free riding."

Curtis expressed a belief that free riding occurred because of the failure of the industry (music or film) to meet the needs and desires of consumers regarding reasonable content, faster releases, format flexibility, and other issues. He was not alone in this viewpoint. Comments such as Curtis's, though, would be met head-on by a variety of experts in the field, including Mike McCurry and Mark McKinnon, the cochairs of Arts + Labs, which is a partnership of technology companies and creative communities.

Discussing the "massive misappropriation of artists' work," McCurry and McKinnon said the argument that the creative community had not done enough to compete with the pirated downloads was akin to arguing "in the physical world . . . that it's OK to steal an iPhone because Apple hasn't figured out how to compete with free."

In a 2009 *Billboard* piece, McCurry and McKinnon stated that almost 90 percent of peak Internet traffic was composed of illegal downloads—which were being practiced by only a very small percentage of Internet users. The editorial detailed the cooperation that had arisen between distribution platforms, such as iTunes, MySpace Music, Hulu, and YouTube, and creative artists and distributors as they moved forward to provide authorized content to consumers.

McCurry and McKinnon discussed the creative industry's work to develop strong photography, animation techniques, and digital compression to better meet the needs and desires of consumers. They pointed out the position of a number of "self-proclaimed Internet rights groups," which were not supporting these new efforts. Some of these groups, they commented, were even going so far as to criticize the decision of YouTube to work in alliance with those who had created content, stating that this activity made the Internet "less free." McCurry is a former White House press secretary; McKinnon is a political consultant who worked for President George W. Bush.

Regardless of where opinion falls on the issues, criminal and civil laws exist to address unauthorized file sharing—as infringement of copyright.

3 The Courts and Congress: Legislation and Court Decisions

CRIMINAL PROSECUTION OR CIVIL CASES RELATED TO Internet piracy can derive from legislation, laws enacted through Congress. They can also derive from court decisions based on existing laws. There are federal laws and state laws, criminal laws and civil laws. When a federal criminal law has been violated, federal prosecutors bring the action on behalf of the U.S. government. When a state criminal law has been violated, state prosecutors bring the action on behalf of the state. Civil cases can be filed by federal or state officials; they can also be filed by individual attorneys on behalf of specific clients.

Civil and Criminal, State and Federal

There are civil and criminal penalties for Internet piracy. Criminal penalties can consist of imprisonment, probation (a period of time during which the criminal's activities are restricted and monitored), fines to be paid to the state or country, and restitution or repayment to a victim, However, criminal charges are not filed for the purpose of gaining money. They are filed for the purpose of criminal prosecution. In other words, criminal prosecution is not to be pursued when the goal is to obtain money—even though a sum might be ordered to be paid as part of a judgment. If the goal is to obtain a monetary amount, a civil case is the type of case that should be filed.

Some civil infractions are handled by state agencies, and some lawsuits are brought by individuals, groups, or businesses. As related to Internet piracy, the goals of civil suits are generally to stop activity and garner monetary judgment.

Legislation

Internet piracy derives from copyright infringement. Clearly, the importance of protecting intellectual property was recognized during the early days of America. In 1790, Congress enacted the first copyright law to protect copyright holders. The law provided protection for only fourteen years; it allowed application for renewal for an additional fourteen. The law was later revised to extend the term of protection.

By 1976, Congress recognized the need to extend the period of protection offered by copyright. Without an extension, many works, such as the early Walt Disney cartoons, would have quickly come into the public domain, which would have allowed use without permission from the copyright holder. Many of these works were still generating substantial income for the copyright holders.

The Copyright Act of 1976 provided for a period of the life of the copyright holder plus fifty years, unless it was a work-for-hire, in which case the period of life was extended to seventy-five years. And in 1998, the Sonny Bono Copyright Term Extension Act modified the fifty-year provision to a seventy-year provision. Bono, a songwriter, musical artist, and actor, had long advocated an extension of this term. After he was elected to Congress, he continued his advocacy in this regard, and the extension resulted.

By 1997, copyright holders and legislators clearly recognized the need to protect types of works that likely had not been imagined by those who founded the country and wrote the initial legis-

Fair Use Doctrine

In the Copyright Act of 1976, Congress included provision for fair use of copyrighted work. Through fair use, a portion of the work might be allowed to be used without constituting copyright infringement. Fair use is often seen in an educational setting, but there is no fair use for poems or songs.

If a use is not "fair use," the party wishing to use the content must obtain permission from the copyright holder prior to use. Contrary to common belief, the legislation, Section 107, does not set out a specific number of words or paragraphs that can be used. And it should be noted that there have been many court cases to interpret the law since its passage. It's also important to recognize that simply providing credit by stating the name of the copyright holder does not mean the use is fair.

These are the considerations set out in the legislation for determining fair use:

1. The purpose and character of the use, including whether such use is of a commercial nature or is for nonprofit educational purposes;
2. The nature of the copyrighted work;
3. The amount and substantiality of the portion used in relation to the copyrighted work as a whole;
4. The effect of the use upon the potential market for, or value of, the copyrighted work.

It is important not to assume a use is fair. There have been entire conferences held to determine fair use in the digital age. Still, the rules are not absolute and crystal clear. It is often considered fair use to quote small portions of a work in a school paper when the paper is scholarly, or for school use only and not for remuneration. Additional uses that are often considered fair use include other scholarly endeavors, such as teaching and research.

When singer-songwriter Sonny Bono *(right)* was elected to Congress, he made it his mission to extend the copyright term of works of art. Before the bill was passed, music legend Johnny Cash *(left)* testified before a House committee on the ill effects of copyright infringement.

lation. The No Electronic Theft Act (NET) was passed to address the concerns. The NET stated that a criminal offense had occurred if a person willfully infringed copyright

1. for purposes of commercial advantage or private financial gain, or

2. by the reproduction or distribution, including by electronic means, during any 180-day period, of one or more copies or phonorecords of one or more copyrighted works, which have a total retail value of more than $1,000.

The act provided for forfeiture and destruction of phonorecords or copies or other items that had been copied in violation of the law. In other words, law enforcement officials could take all the copies from the criminal—regardless of the criminal's investment—and the criminal was not entitled to any compensation. The law also provided penalties for those who knowingly placed false copyright notices—or those who removed actual copyright notices. And the act provided for imprisonment and fines as punishment. The act also contained provisions against counterfeit marks on items, punishable by a civil penalty, or fine.

The Digital Millennium Copyright Act and Liability of ISPs

By the late 1900s, some were clamoring for a law that would hold liable those Internet service providers (ISPs) through whose service illegal activity, such as downloading without a license, had occurred. They believed the huge profits garnered by these companies and the access they provided meant the ISPs should closely monitor activity and be held liable.

But there was a rift of opinion. After all, some reasoned, an ISP couldn't be aware of all activity by all users—and shouldn't the liability lie with those who downloaded, rather than those who provided the means for the communication? Some, such as representatives of the Electronic Frontier Foundation and First Amendment Center, even questioned the constitutionality of holding an ISP liable. After all, they wondered, would it not then follow that a provider of telephone lines and services could be held liable for any illegal activity discussed on a telephone line?

This debate—and other heated debates about digital rights—made their way to Congress, where it was again made clear that legislation needed to catch up to technology—and the Digital Millennium Copyright Act (DMCA) became law in 1998. It would fan the flames of the controversy and provide an avenue for cases against Internet pirates.

Among other provisions, the DMCA limited liability of ISPs

for the act of simply transmitting information; however, it did provide penalties for ISPs that failed to remove material from users' websites that appeared to be the result of copyright infringement. The DMCA also implemented two treaties passed by the World Intellectual Property Organization (WIPO) in 1996. The DMCA was a watershed in the fight against Internet piracy. The act made it illegal to manufacture, sell, or distribute devices designed to crack codes or copy software without license or permission. The law also provided penalties for circumventing antipiracy measures integrated into commercial software. It also included a requirement for webmasters to pay licensing fees to record companies. The legislation did provide for some exceptions and limitations for colleges and universities.

The Digital Theft Deterrence and Copyright Damages Improvement Act

As Internet piracy exploded, so did the call for additional legislation. Congress passed the Digital Theft Deterrence and Copyright Damages Improvement Act of 1999 for the purpose of increasing damages for copyright infringement.

The Family Entertainment and Copyright Act

By 2005, record numbers of bootleggers sat in movie theaters, hunkered down with their own audiovisual equipment, recording the films they viewed—for the purpose of selling bootlegged copies of these films for a profit. Lawmakers recognized this problem, and in 2005, the Family Entertainment and Copyright Act became law. It detailed federal "criminal penalties for unauthorized recording of motion pictures in a motion picture exhibition facility."

While at first blush this law might not seem to be pertinent to Internet piracy, it is important to note that websites have been set up for the purpose of selling such illegal—or bootlegged—films.

Additionally, some criminals sell the bootlegged films on online auction sites. So the criminal sanctions put into place against those who illegally created these films had a clear impact on those who later sold them through the Internet. In addition to federal legislation, most states have also enacted laws against recording a film being displayed in movie theaters.

Court Decisions

The legislation gave rise to criminal prosecutions and civil lawsuits. The greatest initial onslaught of Internet-piracy suits wove its way into the international consciousness through the many cases filed against Napster, the P2P site that allowed free downloads of music without license or permission—and without compensation to those who owned copyright. A number of lawsuits were filed against Napster for copyright infringement by businesses, groups such as Metallica and A & M Records, and individuals. The best-known, though, is *RIAA* v. *Napster*.

RIAA v. Napster

In 1999, the Recording Industry Association of America (RIAA) filed for an injunction against Napster to stop its operations. Through a series of appeals, Napster was first let off the hook and allowed to continue its business operations, but ultimately, Napster declared bankruptcy and went out of business.

Napster later popped up again, but this time it purported to be set up as a legitimate business, charging for downloads. The company was purchased by Best Buy in late 2008 for $121 million.

RIAA v. Verizon Internet Services Inc.

In 2003, the vast majority of teen attitudes, as expressed through a Gallup poll, toward illegally downloading music, illustrated indifference or a belief that the downloading was a good idea. Estimates showed that students at most universities were using more than

RIAA Suits Against Individuals

In 2005, the recording industry filed suits against more than 750 people for file sharing of music over the Internet. By 2009, RIAA had launched accusations of piracy against thousands. Recoveries from each averaged $4,000, most of them settling without a trial. One exception was the case against Jammie Thomas-Rasset. She was a single parent who, it was alleged, had shared twenty-four songs through Kazaa. In 2007, a jury decided for RIAA, awarding nearly $10,000 per song. Some who spoke out on behalf of Thomas-Rasset argued that the penalty would not have been so harsh if she had stolen CDs from a big-box discount store.

The judge tossed out the decision, citing legal grounds regarding instructions to the jury. The judge commented on the disproportionate nature of the award, stating that the defendant had not tried to profit from the act—and that the law should be changed.

RIAA appealed, and the defendant was again found guilty. This time, the award was substantially more than the $10,000 total from the earlier jury. This jury awarded $80,000 for each song, which totaled $1.92 million. Even some of the participants on the RIAA side were surprised. While it could be argued that the fine was so high in an effort to make a point, it could also be stated that Thomas-Rasset had broken the law and was being punished accordingly. The punishment—each time—came from a jury, a group of Thomas-Rasset's peers, so it could also be said that the punishment was fair.

By late 2008, RIAA had shifted its main focus from suits against individuals—which one of its lawyers said had been filed primarily for making other Internet users aware of the illegal nature of the file sharing of copyrighted content—and more in the direction of encouraging ISPs and others to play a greater role in the fight against Internet piracy.

Single mom Jammie Thomas-Rasset was ultimately fined $1.92 million for downloading songs from the Internet for her own enjoyment and her family's—not for making a profit on it. That amount was, of course, far more than she could pay back.

half the university bandwidth for the purpose of uploading and downloading software, films, and songs. The recording industry began to pursue lawsuits against individuals who had downloaded music from sites like Napster.

On a number of college campuses, there were systems that resembled P2P networks, but they existed only on a specific college's internal campus local area network. In 2003, the RIAA filed suits against college students who had been using these networks—and software referred to by the names Direct Connect, Phynd, and Flatlan—and infringed copyright by illegally downloading music. RIAA also moved forward against other individuals for illegal file sharing. Most settled the lawsuits before they proceeded to a trial.

In order to file cases against individuals, it was necessary to have the names of the individuals who had downloaded files. It was easier to identify users through university systems than it was to identify individuals. It was more difficult to obtain names of users from ISPs—and it was particularly difficult for RIAA to obtain records from Verizon. In the spring of 2003, RIAA sued Verizon Internet Services Inc. after Verizon failed to turn over information about subscribers who the RIAA stated had illegally downloaded music.

A provision in the DMCA allows for a speedy subpoena process, which the RIAA had utilized; however, Verizon refused to turn over the information, stating that the First Amendment offered protection. Many groups, including the Electronic Frontier Foundation (EFF) and the American Civil Liberties Union (ACLU), supported Verizon. Their position was that "purported copyright owners should not have the right to violate protected, anonymous speech with what amounts to a single snap of the fingers."

Verizon lost the case. The judge did not view the DMCA as conflicting with First Amendment. The case was appealed, however, and Verizon won the appeal. Verizon was not forced to provide the names of the ISP users.

Metro-Goldwyn-Mayer Inc. et al. v. Grokster Ltd. et al.

By 2005, the *Grokster* case arrived at the U.S. Supreme Court. In the name of the case, the words *et al.* denote that there were numerous parties on both sides of the case. The case would ultimately become known by the names of two of the parties, MGM and Grokster. The plaintiffs, those who filed the case, included MGM, Columbia Pictures, Warner Bros. Entertainment Inc., New Line Cinema Corporation, Twentieth Century Fox Film Corporation, Arista Records, and many others. It's interesting to note that Sony Music Entertainment was also one of the parties bringing the suit, particularly as it had been on the other side in a similar case years earlier. Those who had brought the case against Grokster stated that the defendants had knowingly contributed to massive copyright infringement.

The defendants were P2P companies Grokster and StreamCast. Earlier court decisions regarding Grokster had not ruled its activities illegal. These decisions were partially based on the *Sony Corporation of America* v. *Universal City Studios*, better known as the *Betamax* case, that came before the U.S. Supreme Court in 1984. In that case, Universal City Studios had brought a case against Sony Corporation, which manufactured videotape recorders, or VTRs. Some people were using VTRs to infringe copyright—by copying movies and then selling those copies for a profit. In that case, the Supreme Court ruled that Sony could not be held liable for creating a technology that could be used for the purpose of infringing copyright—as long as there were also legal uses for the technology.

Relying on this decision Grokster attorneys advanced a similar argument in the *MGM* v. *Grokster* case. Gary Shapiro, who was in charge of the Consumer Electronics Association, said that "without the decision in the *Betamax* case, we would never have had iPods. . . . Nor would we have had video recorders, recordable CDs and

Consumer rights activist Michael Petricone argued with Fred Cannon *(right)* about file sharing as they stood outside the Supreme Court on March 29, 2005, while the *Grokster* case was being discussed inside.

DVDs. . . . In fact, the Internet wouldn't exist if Hollywood had its way." The advancement of culture and technology are important aspects of a society, and Shapiro's comments went right to the heart of the impact of court decisions regarding technology and intellectual property. In the *Betamax* case, the decision made it clear that a legal technology being used for illegal purposes was not in the wrong—as long as some legal purpose existed for the technology. Just because there had been illegal activity committed with video recorders, recordable CDs and DVDs, and other technologies, this was no reason to halt the technology and culture. And indeed if the advancements leading to the technology had been stemmed in response to to an earlier illegal use, the CDs and DVDs might never have come into existence at all. If technology were immediately halted every time an illegal use occurred, it could be argued, then culture and technology would be severely stymied.

The EFF, which provided the legal defense for another defendant, StreamCast networks, asked: "As we noted in our arguments before the Court, the case raises a fundamental question at the border between copyright and innovation: When should the distributor of a multi-purpose tool be held liable for the infringements that may be committed by end-users of the tool?" Another argument raised on behalf of Grokster and StreamCast distinguished them from Napster, stating that, as in the *Betamax* case, the Grokster and StreamCast services could be used for legitimate purposes; however, the plaintiffs in the case argued that at least 90 percent of the total services of Grokster and StreamCast constituted copyright infringement.

Those who had brought the case drew a clear distinction between the *Betamax* case—as well as what the EFF referred to as a "distributor of a multi-purpose tool"—and a file-sharing service that had been designed to garner a profit from the taking of songs and films without license or permission. They argued that Grokster and StreamCast could not claim protection under the *Betamax* case "because they intentionally facilitated and actively encouraged and assisted infringement." They also argued: "Grokster's and StreamCast's services do not have 'commercially significant' noninfringing uses." In other words, it was argued that unlike the Sony Betamax VTR, which clearly did have uses that did not violate copyright, such as consumers making videos of family events—the services of Grokster and StreamCast did not meet this test.

The Supreme Court ruled against Grokster and StreamCast, pointing out that to rule otherwise would force "creators of the copyrighted material" to "stand by helplessly as the value of their copyrighted works vanishes." The Court said that support of the arguments on behalf of Grokster and StreamCast "undermines the very foundations of copyright law that the Framers believed critical to motivate the creative activity of authors and artists' . . ." *Metro-Goldwyn-Mayer Studios Inc. et al. v. Grokster, Ltd., et al.*, 545 U. S. 913 (2005).

The Supreme Court had spoken clearly—with a significant impact: P2P networks in the future would have to enter into agreements with copyright holders in order to legally disseminate files, as required by law.

A New Model

It was duly noted that a "business model based on suing your customers" was likely not the ultimate solution to the file sharing problem, so in 2006, Warner Bros. began to embrace the new technology as it announced its plans to collaborate on a network that would offer legal downloads of some of its films.

State Legislation and Prosecution

By 2003, some state laws did exist to address Internet piracy; however, each of these laws had been promulgated by legislators in the individual state. Many lawmakers wanted to see a more uniform set of laws throughout the nation. A similar initiative with the Uniform Commercial Code (UCC) had been very successful years earlier, providing uniform business laws across the nation. However, the UCC did not address computer and digital issues. It was in this environment that the Uniform Computer Information Transactions Act (UCITA) was developed. Indeed, UCITA was initially proposed as an amendment to the UCC, but ultimately stood on its own.

UCITA had been on the drawing board for a number of years, having been initially drafted in 1999—before the demise of Napster. It addressed licenses and regulations for databases, computer software, and digital information. The act was met with great controversy, some considering its language too broad and the power it granted to large commercial software publishers too sweeping. Only two states, Virginia and Maryland, adopted UCITA.

The MPAA advocated adoption of UCITA, as well as legislation it promulgated itself, the Model Communications Security

Legislation, which was dubbed Super-DMCA, referring back to the Digital Millennium Copyright Act of 1998. The initiative was to make existing Internet piracy and cable television theft laws even stronger—through regulating communication services and "unlawful access devices." Those in favor of the law believed it addressed new technology—technology that would soon become commonly used. Those who opposed the law thought it was much too broad. The EFF referred to Super-DMCA as "MPAA's Stealth Attack on Your Living Room."

The EFF stated that the new legislation would criminalize possession of "unlawful communication and access devices," warning: "These measures represent an unprecedented attack on the rights of technologists, hobbyists, tinkerers and the public at large. In essence, these proposals would allow 'communication service providers' to restrict what you can connect to your Internet connection or cable or satellite television lines." The EFF further stated that Super-DMCA would control consumers and undermine innovation.

In 2004, Governor Arnold Schwarzenegger of California signed a state law designed to help fight online piracy. The law required those who disseminate films or music on the Internet to disclose their e-mail addresses. This was unusual, as copyright infringement was generally handled through federal prosecution.

By 2009, the Super-DMCA, or similar laws, had been enacted in Arkansas, Delaware, Florida, Illinois, Maryland, Michigan, Pennsylvania, Virginia, and Wyoming. Though the law passed in Colorado, it was vetoed by the governor.

In 2005, a University of Arizona student, one of the first people in the United States to be prosecuted under a state criminal statute for illegally downloading, pleaded guilty and was sentenced to a deferred jail sentence, two hundred hours of community service, three years' probation, and a fine in the amount of $5,400. He was also ordered to complete a copyright class at the school and to

Actor Jackie Chan *(center)* listened to California governor Arnold Schwarzenegger talk about fighting Internet piracy and respecting property rights during a luncheon in Hong Kong in 2005. Schwarzenegger had recently signed a state law designed to fight such piracy.

refrain from using file-sharing computer programs. Law enforcement officers had found copies of music and movies on his computer. When the movies, including *Matrix Revolutions* and *The Cat in the Hat*, were found on the student's computer, they had not yet been released to the general public, and could be viewed only in movie theaters.

In late 2009, police in New Jersey, North Carolina, California, and Georgia arrested seven people for the crime of selling pirated software from Rosetta Stone, a company that provides technology-based language-learning instruction. Michael Wu, Rosetta Stone's lawyer, said, "The efforts of these police departments and prosecutors' offices should be a clear warning to those who are engaging in software piracy against Rosetta Stone or any other company. . . . Software piracy is theft and we will continue to work vigorously to protect consumers from pirated software by seeking criminal prosecution of those who participate in this fraudulent and illegal activity."

Federal Criminal Prosecution

By the early 2000s, the federal government instituted Operation FastLink, a crackdown on international piracy, "the most far-reaching and aggressive enforcement action ever undertaken against organizations involved in illegal intellectual property piracy over the Internet." The operation was the apex of four separate undercover investigations conducted and coordinated by the Federal Bureau of Investigation (FBI), the FBI Cyber Division, and the U.S. Department of Justice—the Computer Crimes and Intellectual Property Section (CCIPS) of the Criminal Division.

The groups FastLink investigated specialized in the distribution of all types of pirated works, including utility and application software, movies, music, and games. Some of the groups targeted were Class, Project X, Echelon, Kalisto, and Fairlight.

Operation FastLink resulted in the combined efforts of law enforcement in the United States and other countries to conduct worldwide searches for the purpose of dismantling some of the most well-known and prolific online piracy organizations. In a single twenty-four-hour period, more than 120 searches were conducted in twenty-seven states in the United States, as well as in ten foreign countries. As a result, computers, including server storage and distribution hubs, were seized. It was reported that one of the storage and distribution servers in the United States contained approximately 65,000 pirated titles. Early estimates of the value of items seized as a result of FastLink were in excess of $50 million. Estimates of damage to the industry caused by the distribution hubs rose to the hundreds of millions of dollars.

Operations Buccaneer, Bandwidth, and Digital Piratez

By the end of 2001, U.S. agents had executed search warrants throughout the world against virtually every level of criminal organization engaged in illegal software piracy over the Internet. Operations Buccaneer, Bandwidth, and Digital Piratez struck at all aspects of the illegal software, game, and movie trade, often referred to as warez scene. Robert S. Mueller, director of the FBI, said, "The execution of these search warrants marks the completion of the most extensive software piracy undercover investigation that the FBI has participated in to date, and should send the message that trafficking in stolen goods—whether the property is in physical or electronic form—is a serious crime, and will be prosecuted."

By 2005, another operation, Site Down, was initiated through the U.S. Department of Justice's Computer Crimes and Intellectual Property Section. And by 2006, Operations Site Down and FastLink were showing a substantial impact—and tremendous success in criminal convictions. By 2007, dozens of defendants had been convicted of felony copyright infringement thanks to the work of Operation FastLink.

Examples of Federal Criminal Sentences Resulting from Operation FastLink

Houtan Yaghmai, who law enforcement officers stated was known as a courier of illegal software, movie, music, and game trade, was sentenced to one year in prison for being involved in an Internet piracy ring—for illegally obtaining copyrighted content and providing it to other members of an underground group, a group operating outside accepted business procedures.

George C. Stoutenburgh of Colorado was sentenced to one year and one day of federal imprisonment for his involvement in an Internet software piracy ring. Stoutenburgh was a site operator who owned and operated an online computer hub. Among the items illegally distributed were music, software, movies, and games. As explained in a press release from the U.S. Department of Justice:

Such warez distribution sites ultimately supply the for-profit criminal distribution networks that cost the copyright industry billions of dollars each year. Although pirated software titles are initially distributed only to a closed group, the titles quickly filter down to commercial distribution sites and peer-to-peer networks within hours. Illegal warez copies of software or movies are then easily and cheaply converted to optical discs and distributed throughout the world from factories in Asia and elsewhere. Spammers regularly advertise cheap software that can be downloaded from websites or shipped from overseas, usually bearing the signature mark of the warez group that released it.

Supporters of the Pirate Bay website demonstrated in Stockholm, Sweden, against a new government antipiracy law.

4 Internet Piracy in Other Countries: Impact on the United States

TODAY, THE INTERNET IS A PART OF OUR DAILY EXISTENCE. People in America and across the world take advantage of "the net" in daily communication, recreation, and retrieval of information— from the most basic to the sophisticated and complex. The Internet is so integrated into daily life, it is easy to forget it became a common household tool only during the past decade.

As with any vast social or technological change, the Internet has catalyzed a host of legal questions and dilemmas. The United States is only one of the countries across the world facing and tackling issues related to Internet piracy. While America has repeatedly proved itself to be a legal pioneer, its policies and processes also have a long history of being informed by those of other countries. In order to consider how the current legal struggles in other parts of the world may affect the future of antipiracy laws in the United States, we must examine the recent developments in those countries.

Pirate Bay: Sweden

Law enforcement officers from the United States and around the world have cooperated in investigations of Internet piracy, a crime whose tentacles stretch through and around many nations, often hiding behind smoke screens afforded them by technology. The experiences of people in nations around the world are not so very different from the experiences of people in the United States.

At the core of the battle against Internet piracy, there exists a hotbed of moral argument. Perhaps nowhere is this more pronounced than in Sweden. In 2006, a new political party, the Pirate Party, was formed in Sweden. It has grown into one of the largest, most influential parties in the country, and it has inspired similar parties throughout the world. A major tenet of the party is to reform copyright laws and essentially abolish patent laws. The party advocates making file sharing legal, stating that the content available through the Internet should be free to all. Culture is of paramount importance; so is knowledge, and the Internet is a vast depository of both. The Pirate Party states that file sharing is to be celebrated, rather than criminalized. The party holds that all copying should be legal for non-commercial use. And for commercial use, they believe that copyrights should be limited to a term of five years. It is the position of the Pirate Party that if the copyright holder has failed to derive sufficient income from the work within five years, it will not do so at a later time.

With the election in 2009 of a member of the Pirate Party, the legal battle against Internet piracy reached a point of major contention with those citizens who argued that file sharing is not morally wrong. Indeed, the founders of Pirate Bay (not owned by the Pirate Party), one of the largest and most popular file-sharing sites in the world, seem to have an almost comical attitude toward potential legal repercussions. When faced with the threat of legal action from a U.S. film company, the founders posted on their website a response loaded with obscenities and implications that the lawyers representing the film company were "morons"—and that their efforts to crack down on the site or its founders would be fruitless.

A European case in 2009 focused on Pirate Bay, which was

said by some to be "one of the world's largest and most notorious file-sharing hubs," exchanging millions of files daily. The site did not store files; instead, it served the role of huge clearinghouse or directory. As a directory, it pointed users to the location of desired files on BitTorrent, which was a file sharing network.

The investigation, which began in 2003, lasted five years—and culminated in charges filed against four men—Gottfrid Svartholm Warg, Fredrik Neij, Peter Sunde, and Carl Lundstrom. A portion of the defense focused on the claim that Pirate Bay was much like Google, or any other search engine, in that it facilitated links related to search parameters. After all, the Pirate Bay defendants argued, search engines do sometimes return hits that consist of sites with illegal content.

The Swedish court did not agree. The court first found that file sharing of illegal files had occurred. Then the court determined that the defendants, acting as a team to operate Pirate Bay, were aware of the transmission of content that violated copyright—but that they still continued the service. In 2009, all four defendants were found guilty of breaking copyright law. They were sentenced to one year in prison and payment of damages that totaled approximately $3.6 million, a tidy sum, but not even close to the $17.5 million in damages and interest sought by entertainment companies such as Sony Music Entertainment, Warner Bros., Columbia Pictures, and EMI Music.

The decision was hailed as a tremendous victory for those in the music industry. One of the defendants, Sunde, has been quite vocal about the sentencing. He said he found the conviction "bizarre," and he remarked: "We can't pay and we wouldn't pay. Even if I had the money I would rather burn everything I owned, and I wouldn't even give them the ashes." Such comments from those associated with Pirate Bay have not been unusual. In fact, they have grown to be anticipated by those familiar with Pirate Bay.

Pirate Bay had gone the way of file-sharing services in the

United States, such as Napster and Grokster. It was clear that the international community was prepared to move forward to address copyright infringement through Internet piracy. And with the recent developments in the Pirate Bay case, the Swedish government seems to be following in footsteps of the United States—a step that will likely further reinforce U.S. legislation and court decisions.

Germany

The social argument that file sharing should not be illegal is also quite visible in German politics, with so-called pirates becoming part of the government, just as they have in Sweden. The Swedish Pirate Party won 7.1 percent of the national vote in June 2009. Perhaps Germany has yet to see such a number, but the German Pirate Party has been shaking traditional government by winning city council seats across the country. It is theorized that German youths are so disillusioned with their government that they are willing to rally around a party that takes a strong stance on only one issue—Internet piracy.

Three-Strikes Legislation in France

In the spring of 2009, the French National Assembly did an about-face on a proposed law promulgated to punish those who violated protection-of-intellectual-property laws through Internet downloads of items such as movies and music. In April of 2009, the National Assembly had voted against such a law, but in May, the law was approved. An agency was to be created to communicate with those who violated copyright through illegal downloads. A first warning would be sent. If it were ignored, a second warning would be sent. If the second warning were ignored, the individual's Internet access would be revoked.

After passing in the French National Assembly, the law moved to the French Constitutional Council. There, it was revised. Lawmakers were concerned about an agency being granted the right

Graduated Response in the International Community

The graduated-response approach proposed by the Recording Industry Association of America (RIAA), designed to incorporate the cooperation of Internet service providers (ISPs), was proposed in New Zealand, France, and Britain. The idea was not well received in New Zealand and was essentially tossed out. In France, the idea was viewed as a presumption of guilt, rather than innocence, so the idea didn't move forward there, either. And in Britain, it was not thought advisable to cut off access, which would have been required of ISPs in certain conditions under the graduated-response approach. The European Parliament had concerns over sanctions that might be implemented without judicial oversight.

to make a decision as serious as suspending service, so the Council amended the law to mandate that the decision to suspend would be made by a judge. While some lawmakers were worried that people could be held responsible for the actions of others who were using their Internet connection, other lawmakers, such as Chairman Jacques Legendre of the Committee on Culture, Education, and Communication, stated that the law was an important protection for creative works and those who created them.

Ireland has passed a law similar to France's three-strikes law. Similar laws are pending—or their introduction is being promulgated—in other countries.

Demonstrators from many different European countries marched together in France to protest a European Union project that would more closely regulate Internet piracy.

While much headway has been made in the fight against Internet piracy in the United States, the question as to whether American lawmakers would be interested in similar legislation remains. Only time will tell whether the United States goes the way of the three-strikes law, but American constitutional issues and due-process rights make passage of such a law highly unlikely.

The IFPI and Pirated Files in Europe

By 2004, the International Federation of the Phonographic Industry (IFPI) shared a study identifying an increase of awareness of legal downloading sites in Europe. The pirate files on the Internet had dropped. IFPI chairman and CEO Jay Berman said, "Today's results show that litigation, combined with the rollout of new legal online music services, is having a real impact on people's attitudes on illegal file sharing and this in turn is affecting levels of file sharing activity." The IFPI noted a decrease in the number of illegal music files on the Internet.

Britain

While Britain was considering legislation that could block Internet access, a plan was put in place that would further consider the matter, but would not allow Internet access to be blocked prior to 2011. Many opposed this long waiting period. Additionally, Britain did not favor the three-strikes approach, expressing an interest in encouraging cooperation between ISPs and the entertainment industry to move forward together to fight Internet piracy.

China

It is estimated that the United States entertainment industry loses millions of dollars each year because of Internet piracy. While it can be argued that individuals in many countries engage in Internet piracy as a result of consumers' unwillingness to spend money

This screenshot was taken in Chongqing, China, on December 14, 2009. It shows the BitTorrent P2P download website tiantianbt.com. Soon after, the government disabled all media downloads.

on forms of entertainment, Internet piracy in some nations, such as China, also has ties to government censorship.

The Chinese government has long banned foreign television shows and films, identifying this action as "necessary to protect public morals." Ironically, Chinese Internet sites are some of the easiest portals for gaining access to free Western entertainment.

Prior to 2009, there had been little cooperation forthcoming from the Chinese government to crack down on Internet pirates. The reasons for this are not entirely clear; however, the theory may be that if Chinese citizens have access to Western entertainment entirely revoked, they will increase pressure on their government to lift censorship laws.

The Chinese government recently took a decisive turn when the China Internet Video Anti-Piracy Alliance—composed of Chinese portals, as well as foreign-rights owners like the Motion Picture Association of America—announced that it would be taking legal action against multiple violators.

More than five hundred accusations of Internet piracy were declared against Youku, one of the most popular Chinese websites. The action called for Western companies to be compensated by the websites for importing their materials. The sites would then be able to charge users for content. While the first suit filed by the alliance claims damages only against China-based companies, winning the case would have a substantial impact on the future of Internet piracy in China and its effects on the United States.

In December of 2007, the Beijing Higher People's Court held that Yahoo! China had violated the law "by committing mass copyright infringement." And by early 2009, Yahoo! China had failed to comply with provisions of the ruling.

In early 2008, the recording industry stated it would implement new tactics "to try to develop a music business in China based on respect rather than blatant violation of copyright laws."

Many months of negotiations had failed to produce progress, so legal proceedings were filed against Baidu, which was China's largest Internet company. Two other Internet companies, Sohu and associated Sogou, were also made part of legal proceedings.

The IFPI represents the recording industry throughout the world. IFPI chairman and chief executive John Kennedy stated, "The music industry in China wants partnership with the technology companies—but you cannot build partnership on the basis of systemic theft of copyrighted music and that is why we have been forced to take further actions." He identified China as having "potentially the largest online music-buying public in the world."

At the beginning of 2008, a study from the IFPI stated that "piracy was responsible for 99 percent of the Chinese market." Many had been articulating serious concerns about the Chinese attitude toward Internet piracy. In Cannes, France, a Chinese spokesman met with reporters to discuss the issue. Zhang Xin Jian, the deputy director-general of the Ministry's Markets Administration, said, "I am not sure of the accuracy of 99 percent, but I still feel this is a very grave situation in China right now." He outlined a determination of his government to tighten controls and move forward toward prosecution of those responsible for infractions. In September of 2009, it was announced that the Chinese Ministry of Culture had ordered search engines to offer links only to licensed music sources.

Fight Piracy with a Tax?

One tiny island has come up with an alternative to arming itself with laws to prosecute its citizens for Internet piracy. On the Isle of Man, a self-governing entity between Ireland and Great Britain, the government has imposed a tax equivalent to approximately $1.40 upon each citizen. The tax is to be paid to recording companies to compensate for citizens' unlimited music downloads. While a similar effort in France failed in 2006, after fierce arguments by recording companies, some say that this is not only the most practical way, but even the only effective way to deal with a pandemic of file sharing.

Peer-to-Peer—PTPTV?

In 2004, it seemed as though aspects of the defunct Napster were about to appear in Germany, where a software engineer, Guido Ciburski, and his business partner, Petra Bauersachs, had been working on software that could give streaming video on the Internet a Napster twist—a new file-sharing enterprise called Cybersky. One feature of the site? It would allow users to upload video, which could then be accessed through live feed. The Cybersky site has a disclaimer explaining that the swapping of pay TV is allowed only with permission of the network. Legally, the question is whether the site will retransmit programs that are copyrighted. If so, such transmission is illegal unless permission is obtained.

Guido Ciburski is no stranger to innovation—or litigation. He and his partner developed and sold a device for televisions that recorded programs and skipped advertisements. Broadcasters sued, but lost. Ciburski seems ready to put the boxing gloves back on, saying of his new Cybersky: "What, are we going to say, 'We're scared of how people will react,' and put it back in our drawer so that someone else can come along and do it?" While there was an injunction issued against Cybersky—an order to cease operations—the injunction was lifted.

Programs with similar PTPTV products were developed in Sweden, by the founders of the Internet telephone software Skype, and in China. The Swedish product, developed by Niklas Zennstrøm and Janus Friis, was dubbed Joost. In the United States, the product available was Miro, which had originally been developed as the Democracy Player in China by the Participatory Culture Foundation, an organization that describes itself as "a founder of the Open Video Alliance, a coalition of organizations, companies, and individuals that are working to create open tools, workflows, licensing systems for online video." On its Website, Miro was described as an "Open-source, non-profit video player and podcast client." It was operating in the United States in 2010. While Cybersky, Joost, and Miro had similar PTPTV products and services, their products and methods of delivery varied. As these systems continue to grow, the likely legal tests will be interesting to monitor.

Rapid Advancement of Technology

The argument that Internet piracy around the world is unstoppable is increasingly gaining steam. Some recording businesses, perhaps in recognition of this idea, have already agreed to proposed royalty rates for online streaming and digital downloads. Willie Kavanagh, chairman of the Irish Recorded Music Association, cautions that careful analysis must be paid to such an arrangement in order to ensure that record companies are indeed being compensated adequately.

Bob Lefsetz, a California music industry analyst, observes that technology is advancing threefold: "The bottom line is you are going to have instant delivery of everything you want, whenever you want." With increased ease and usage of illegal downloads and illegal streaming video providing music, movies, and TV shows, laws could be implemented effectively at a comparable rate.

5 Internet Piracy: The Future

THE RISE OF THE INTERNET IN THE PAST DECADES HAS created an indelible impact on the daily lives of Americans and others around the world. It has given rise to new avenues for business, entertainment, and social connection that might have previously been inconceivable. Social networking sites such as Twitter and Facebook are an integral part of many people's lives. This steep ascent into our usual routines has also produced a new market for illegal activity. Internet piracy has become rampant. It is projected that the industry will continue to feel the effects of piracy, even with the huge strides in combating it.

The easy accessibility of broadband Internet, along with the ability of a wider range of the population to afford high-speed access, has contributed to piracy, as it has led to a greater ability to download large entertainment files. Broadband is a communications network that allows accessibility to a variety of sites for many users. Many agree that college campuses will continue to be prime hotspots for Internet piracy, even though the problem has been addressed through lawsuits, criminal charges, and school intervention. At their university information and technology services departments, students often have access to the latest and fastest broadband Internet. The social nature of the college campus will likely continue to fuel the rampant piracy and widespread sharing of entertainment sources from the Internet.

Internet piracy has clearly had an impact on society, and the

iTunes and Hulu and Spotify— Oh, My!

Hulu began as a joint venture between NBC Universal and News Corporation. Videos proliferated on the Internet, and clips were being downloaded at an astronomical rate. Clearly, there was profit to be made. Hulu offers fast and easy—and legal—access to a number of TV shows. And much of the profit comes from advertising.

iTunes, an Apple offering, provides legal downloads of music. Spotify is being hailed by some as the British equivalent of iTunes. Spotify is a legal service, but it differs somewhat from iTunes in that it provides a huge library of music that can be played in real time. While Spotify's offerings are not as expansive as those of iTunes, when Spotify first popped onto the music scene, its library was substantial.

Most consumers receive the Spotify service for free—with twenty seconds of advertisements between songs every thirty minutes. To circumvent the ads, subscribers can pay a monthly or daily subscription fee. Because consumers listen to the music in real time, they are not downloading, so there is no downloading piracy issue.

It is likely that legal services such as iTunes, Hulu, and Spotify will continue to grow well into the future.

3	☑ Steal My Kisses	○	3:43 Alanis Morris...	○ Jagged Little ...
4	☑ Tears In Heaven	○	4:05 Ben Harper	○ Burn To Shine
5	☑ Layla	○	4:36 Eric Clapton	○ Unplugged
6	☑ Like A Virgin	○	4:46 Eric Clapton	○ Unplugged
7	☑ Material Girl	○	3:11 Madonna	○ The Immacul...
8	☑ Come As You Are	○	3:53 Madonna	○ The Immacul...
9	☑ Nothingman	○	4:13 Nirvana	○ MTV Unplugg...
10	☑ Losing My Religion	○	4:35 Pearl Jam	○ Vitalogy
11	☑ Scar Tissue	○	4:29 R.E.M.	○ Out of Time
12	☑ Californication	○	3:37 Red Hot Chili ...	○ Californication
13	☑ Maria Maria	○	5:21 Red Hot Chili ...	○ Californication
14	☑ Building A Mystery	●	4:22 Santana	○ Supernatural
			4:07 Sarah McLach...	○ Surfacing
15	☑ If it Makes You Happy	○	5:23 Sheryl Crow	○ Sheryl Crow
16	☑ Brown Eyed Girl	○	3:05 Van Morrison	○ Best Of Van ...
17	☑ B To Shine	○	3:34 Ben Harper	○ Burn To Shine
18	☑ ven	○	5:17 Ben Harper	○ Burn To Shine
19	Home Rol	○	3:40 G. Love & Spe...	○ Has Gone Co...
20		○	5:48 Morcheeba	○ Big Calm
22		○	2:54 Pearl Jam	○ Vitalogy
23	nce	○	4:04 Sarah McLach...	○ Surfacing
		○	4:32 Van Morrison	○ Best Of Van ...

Apple CEO Steve Jobs stands in front of a projection of the iTunes website at the launch of the iTunes Music Store in Europe.

question looms as to how to respond to this activity. Some label piracy an illegal activity; others further call into question the morality of stealing intellectual property.

Given the perpetuation of Internet piracy that can occur on university campuses, attention has turned toward the role universities can play in curbing piracy. Educating students about the moral and legal implications of Internet piracy will likely continue to be a focus of college and university administrations as the debate about the morality of file sharing continues.

Taking the Internet Piracy Discussion to School

By 2006, Jon Dudas of the U.S. Patent Office was speaking to students in elementary schools to spread the word about intellectual property rights and Internet piracy. He explained to the young students: "You wouldn't take a CD off the shelf without paying for it. . . . And you shouldn't get music on the Internet without paying for it."

Some go so far as to say that the future of preventing Internet piracy should begin much earlier in the education system—with increased funding for music education in public schools, to aid children's understanding of the impact of Internet piracy on musicians and others who do creative work.

It's interesting to note that some theorists still question whether to fight Internet piracy at all; instead, they argue, we should move forward to accommodate Internet piracy. They suggest that embracing Internet piracy and file sharing may actually produce a more desirable result. Some say that downloading files can help buyers identify their favorite products more easily and actually encourages sales. Others in the field state that studying optimal pricing to compete with Internet piracy may help in countering the proliferation and effects of piracy.

In 2007, the popular band Radiohead conducted a social experiment of sorts. It resulted in something many viewed as a microcosm of views on Internet piracy. Radiohead released its seventh album to fans at a "you-name-it" CD price; fans could digitally download the new album from the website for the price they chose, one option being $0. This experiment was groundbreaking in the field and seen as a direct response to the changing face of music use and access.

Response was varied, from listeners paying nothing and expressing the sentiment that the band didn't need the money to others paying what was considered fair market value, saying that people should pay for their art. And it was discovered that despite the offer to download the CD for free via the website, some users still downloaded the album illegally from another site. Why? Many cite the ease of access. These findings may point to an even larger issue in fighting Internet piracy—that today's generation thinks music is "free."

In 2007, the popular band Radiohead performed a groundbreaking experiment in music pricing and accessibility.

The Future of Internet Piracy of Software

Antipiracy efforts remain on the forefront of the software agenda.

Software companies look to new distribution agreements, including "cloud computing," which consists of distribution models such as bundling computers with broadband services and delivering software-as-a-service. It is believed this will enhance the fight against piracy. Because the software will be delivered to the user, the revenue to the copyright holder will have already been addressed before the user buys it.

Vendor legalization provides for agreements with large customers to provide software at volume discounts—to be exchanged for pirated software. The BSA states that this has been effective and will likely be incorporated into future efforts.

As explained by the BSA, vendor agreements with original equipment manufacturers are agreements to preload software onto hardware systems before they are shipped. Such efforts have been successful in the past and are expected to continue.

The future of responding to Internet piracy will involve a dynamic combination of governmental protection policies and regulation, a shift in the population's understanding of the morality of piracy, and a change in the way entertainment industries market and sell their products.

Book Scanning

By the 2000s, the first devices were developed and released for commercial creation and reading of digital files of books. New concerns were born regarding the possibility of illegal book downloads that might arise in the future. Some pondered the whole Napster debacle, wondering if something similar might be on the horizon for books.

In 2004, Google developed Google Book Search, which included more than 10 million books. The books had been scanned and could be accessed through a search engine. Google had not, though, obtained permission from the authors of these books prior to scanning them and making them available.

In a National Public Radio interview in September of 2009 with Google cofounder Sergey Brin, journalist Laura Sydell stated: "Google cofounder Sergey Brin defends this active ambition by citing the fires at the Library of Alexandria in ancient Egypt. Historians believe those fires destroyed one of the ancient world's greatest repositories of knowledge. . . . It also happens to be Google's corporate mission to make all of the world's knowledge searchable."

Sergey replied: "The books were a very important part of that, and so much of the wisdom of humanity is captured in that."

There is an argument that Google was, indeed, providing an important service and that remuneration was not due to authors or publishers. After all, it is possible to walk into a library and read or check out an entire book, free of charge. There is also an argument to be made that the income of publishing houses and many

authors rests primarily in book sales, including to libraries, and they lose income when a book is available for free on the Internet.

A copyright class-action case, a case on behalf of a group of plaintiffs, was filed against Google. While Google denied the claims, the case was settled, with the possibility of opting in—for a cash amount—for authors whose books had been scanned, or opting out, which would mean the author would not be tied to the settlement and could file a lawsuit against Google. "For books that enter Google Books through the Library Project, what you see depends on the book's copyright status. We respect copyright law and the tremendous creative effort authors put into their work. If the book is in the public domain and therefore out of copyright, you can page through the entire book and even download it and read it offline. But if the book is under copyright, and the publisher or author is not part of the Partner Program, we only show basic information about the book, similar to a card catalog, and, in some cases, a few snippets—sentences of your search terms in context. The aim of Google Books is to help you discover books and assist you with buying them or finding a copy at a local library. It's like going to a bookstore and browsing—with a Google twist."

What the Future Holds

It will be crucial for legislators and policymakers to continue researching and implementing the most effective policies and laws to curb rampant piracy. Likewise, schools must continue to address the issue of piracy on an administrative level so schools educate students about the effects of Internet piracy. And businesses will likely continue to adapt to the new "instant gratification" culture by providing their products in the most convenient way possible.

What does the future hold? At present, the iPad is only one of several devices available for the downloading of books. For the most part, books that have copyright protection must be paid for before they are read, but . . . with music as an example, will a change in the way people pay for books be far behind?

It is clear the creative industry is in transition. Bands, fans, record labels, and government are all struggling to contend with a drastically and rapidly changing market. With the new generation of fans growing up in what is sometimes perceived as a "free music" society, the industry faces the challenge of combating this notion—and the government is called on to enforce laws governing sometimes-difficult-to-identify infringements. To fight or accommodate Internet piracy? Only time will tell.

Notes

Chapter 1

p. 13, "Internet piracy is the downloading . . . ": Motion Picture Association of America, "What is Internet Piracy?" Motion Picture Association, 2005, www.mpaa.org/piracy_internet.asp.

p. 13, "Broadly defined, piracy is . . . ": James Greenberg and William Triplett, "Internet Theft: How It Happens and Why It Matters," *DGA Quarterly* (Fall 2009).

p. 13, "Software piracy is the unauthorized . . . ": Business Software Alliance, "What is Software Piracy?" Business Software Alliance, 2000–2009, www.bsa.org/country/Anti-Piracy/What-is-Software-Piracy.aspx.

p. 13, "Intellectual property . . . refers to creations of the mind . . . ": World Intellectual Property Organization, "About Intellectual Property" World Intellectual Property Organization, www.ompi.ch/about-ip/en/.

p. 16, "visibly shaken . . . ": McClure, Dave. "Copyright wars 2001: Will ISPs survive?" *Boardwatch*, October 2000.

p. 17, "Jason Everett Spatafore, also known as Disman . . . ": U.S. Department of Justice. *Man Pleads Guilty to Internet piracy of Star Wars Film*, Northern District of California, December 15, 2000, www.justice.gov/criminal/cybercrime/spataforeplea.htm.

p. 17, "one report stated he earned a total . . . ": Jason Thompson, "Copyright on Trial," *StreamingMedia.com*, May 30, 2001, www.streamingmedia.com/article.asp?id=7450

p. 17, "Spatafore noted that the ISP . . . ": Thompson, "Copyright on Trial," www.streamingmedia.com/article.asp?id=7450.

p. 20, "Many college kids think . . . ": Peter Galuszka, "The War over Internet Piracy," *Black Issues in Higher Education*, March 11, 2004.

p. 20, "By 2004, the recording industry . . . ": Galuszka, "The War over Internet Piracy."

p. 21, "Madonna's manager stated . . . ": John Borland, "Unreleased Madonna single slips onto Net," *CNET News*, CNET, June 1, 2005, http://news.cnet.com/2100-1023-241341.html.

p. 22, "The people who are on the board of directors . . . ": Steven Levy, "The Noisy War Over Napster," *Newsweek*, June 5, 2000.

p. 23, "Consumers simply do not see bootlegged movies as illegal . . . ": Greenberg and Triplett, "Internet Theft."

p. 23, "stated that piracy of TV shows . . . ": Daisy Whitney, "As Piracy Climbs, TV Takes Up Arms," *TV Week*, May 18, 2009.

Chapter 2

p. 26, "I like what's going on . . . ": Chris Matyszczyk, "Shakira says file sharing is just fine," *CNET News*, CNET, October 21, 2009, http://news.cnet.com/8301-17852_3-10380995-71.html.

p. 26, "Ed O'Brien . . . ": Andre Paine, "Elton John Joins File sharing Debate," *Billboard.biz, Billboard*, 2010. www.billboard.biz/bbbiz/content_display/industry/e3i7c69fb437bbee15e5cc93a0a7d2b99.

p. 26, "The last thing we want to be doing . . . ": Paine, "Elton John Joins File sharing Debate," www.billboard.biz/bbbiz/content_display/industry/e3i7c69fb437bbee15e5cdc93a07a7d2b99.

p. 26, "the leading civil liberties group . . .": Electronic Frontier Foundation, www.eff.org.

p. 26, "copyright litigation can also . . . ": William K. Norton, "Internet & First Amendment: copyright, P2P & Google," *First Amendment Center*, June 10, 2009, www.firstamendmentcenter.org/speech/internet/topic.aspx?topic=file_sharing.

p. 27, "sales of CDs . . ": Jonathan Band, "The Copyright Paradox," *The Brookings Review*, Winter 2001.

p. 27, "free Internet downloads are good . . . ": Janis Ian, "The Internet Debacle: An Alternative View." *Performing Songwriter* magazine, May 2009, www.janisian.com/articles-perfsong/internet debacle.pdf.

p. 28, "Ian wrote that . . . ": Janis Ian, "FALLOUT: a follow up to The Internet Debate." *janisian.com*, August 1, 2002, www.janisian. com/articles-perfsong/Fallout%20-%20rev%2011-23-05.pdf.

p. 30, "In an interview . . . ": Anthony Bruno, "Billboard.biz Q&A: Former RIAA CEO Rosen Talks Napster." *billboardbiz. com* Billboard, June 1, 2009. www.billboard.biz/bbbiz/search/ article_display.jsp?vnu_content_id=1003978498.

p. 31, "said the motion picture worldwide . . . ": Brian Braiker, "Viral Video," *Newsweek*, June 15, 2007. www.newsweek.com/id/33938.

p. 31, "a 'huge threat' to studios and filmmakers. . . ": www.archive. org/stream/MpaaPiracyReport/LeksummarympaRevised_djvu.txt.

p. 32, "organized crime . . . ": Motion Picture Association of America, www.mpaa.org/piracy_Piracy_organized_Crime.asp.

p. 32, "has workers numbering 750,000 . . . ": Motion Picture Association of America, www.mpaa.org/piracy_Economies.asp.

p. 32, "voice of the world's software industry . . . ": Business Software Alliance, www.bsa.org/country/BSA%20and%20Members. aspx.

p. 33, "BSA shut down more than . . . ": U.S. Federal News Service, "BSA Raises the Stakes in the Fight Against Software Piracy Online, Extends $1 Million Reward to Qualified Reports of Internet Piracy," Washington, D.C., April 3, 2008.

p. 33, "BSA implemented a $1 million . . . ": U.S. Federal News Service, "BSA Raises the Stakes."

p. 34, "The BSA reported prosecution of . . . ": Business Software Alliance, "Faces of Internet Piracy," Business Software Alliance, 2009 http://global.bsa.org/faces/index.html

p. 36, "We hope AT&T recognizes . . . ": Sanford Nowlin, "AT&T slammed over piracy plan," *San Antonio Express-News*, June 15, 2007.

p. 36, "AT&T and its media industry . . . ": Nowlin, "AT&T slammed over piracy plan."

p. 37, "a Washington, DC, based . . . ": Public Knowledge, www.publicknowledge.org.

p. 37, "which he referred to as free-riding.": Chelsea McNutt, "The Problem of Internet Piracy Gains Attention," *VOANews*, Voice of America, August 28, 2007, www.voanews.com/english/archive/2007-08/2007-08-28-voa21.cfm?moddate=2007-08-28.

p. 37, "expressed a belief that free-riding occurred . . . ": McNutt, "The Problem of Internet Piracy Gains Attention," www.voanews.com/english/archive/2007-08/2007-08-28-voa21.cfm?moddate=2007-08-28.

p. 37, "In the physical world . . . ": Mike McCurry and McKinnon, "Getting to Yes," *Billboard.biz* Billboard, May 9, 2009. www.billboard.biz/bbbiz/search/article_display.jsp?vnu_content_id=1003968344&imw=Y.

p. 36, "stated that 90 percent of peak . . ." McCurry and McKinnon, "Getting to Yes," May 9, 2009.

Chapter 3

p. 46, *RIAA* v. *Napster; RIAA* v. *Napster, Inc.*, No. C 99-05183 MHP, 2000 WL 573136 and *RIAA Napster, Inc.*, 239 F.3d 1004 (9th Cir. 2001).

p. 46, "purchased by Best Buy . . . ": Endgadget, www.engadget.com/2008/09/15/best-buy-acquires-napster-for-121-million.

p. 47, "In 2005, the recording industry filed . . . ": *Los Angeles Times*, March 1, 2005.

p. 47, "Jammie Thomas-Rasset . . ." ": Larry Oakes, "Brainerd mom takes on music industry." *Star Tribune* (Minneapolis, MN), Oct. 3, 2007. Greg Sandoval, "Court orders Jammie Thomas to pay $192 million," *cnet news,* June 18, 2009, http://news.cnet.com/8301-1023_3-10268199-93.html.

p. 49, *RIAA* v. *Verizon Internet Services, Inc.*, 351 F.3d 1229 (D.C. Cir. 2003).

p. 50, *Metro-Goldwyn-Mayer Studios Inc. et al.* v. *Grokster, Ltd., et al.*, 545 U. S. 913 (2005).

p. 50, "business model based on . . .": "Fighting Internet Piracy—Plan B," *Wall Street Journal,* May 15, 2006.

p. 50, "we definitely wouldn't have had . . . ": Steven Levy, "A Very Dangerous Supremes Rerun," *Newsweek,* April 4, 2005.

p. 52, "As we noted in our arguments . . . ": Electronic Frontier Foundation, http://w2.eff.org/IP/P2P/MGM_v_Grokster.

p. 52, "argued that at least 90 percent . . . ":*MGM. et al.* v. *Grokster, Ltd., et al.*, 545 U.S. 913 (2005).

p. 54, "The EFF referred to Super-DMCA . . .": Fred von Lohmann, "State 'Super-DMCA' Legislation: MPAA's Stealth Attack on Your Living Room," Electronic Frontier Foundation, March 10, 2009. http://w2.eff.org/IP/DMCA/states/200304_sdmca_eff_analysis.php.

p. 54, "In 2005, a University of Arizona . . . ": Beth DeFalco, "Teen convicted under Internet piracy law," *USA Today,* March 7, 2005. www.usatoday.com/tech/news/techpolicy/2005-03-07-az-teen-downloader-convicted_x.htm.

p. 55, "In late 2009, police in . . . ": "Rosetta Stone Commends Law Enforcement for Seven Piracy Arrests," *Business Wire,* October 19, 2009. www.businesswire.com/portal/site/google/?ndmViewId=news_view&newsId=20091019005836&newsLang=en.

p. 56, "the most far-reaching . . . ": U.S. Department of Justice, *Justice Department Announces International Internet Piracy Sweep,* Washington, DC, April 22, 2004. www.justice.gov/archive/opa/pr/2005/June/05_crm_353.htm.

p. 56, "The groups FastLink investigated . . . ": U.S. Department of Justice, *Justice Department Announces International Internet Piracy Sweep,*www.justice.gov/archive/opa/pr/2005/June/05_crm_353.htm.

p. 56, "Operation FastLink resulted in . . . ": U.S. Department of Justice, *Justice Department Announces International Internet Piracy Sweep*, www.justice.gov/archive/opa/pr/2005/June/05_crm_353.htm.

p. 57, "By the end of 2001, . . . ": U.S. Department of Justice, *Federal Law Enforcement Targets International Internet Piracy Syndicates*, Washington, D.C. December 11, 2001. www.justice.gov/opa/pr/2001/December/01_crm_643.htm.

p. 58, "Houtan Yaghmai . . . ": U.S. Department of Justice, *Defendant Sentenced to One Year in Federal Prison as Part of Internet Piracy Crackdown*, Western District of North Carolina, November 1, 2007, www.justice.gov/criminal/cybercrime/yaghmaiSent.htm.

p. 59, "George C. Soutenburgh . . . ": U.S. Department of Justice, *Defendant Sentenced to One Year and One Day in Federal Prison as Part of Internet Piracy Crackdown*, U.S. Attorney's Office for the Western District of North Carolina, April 24, 2007, www.justice.gov/usao/ncw/press/fastlink.html.

Chapter 4

p. 62, "posted a response on their Website . . . ": Cable News Network, "Four Found Guilty in Landmark Pirate Bay Case," *Cnn.com*. April 18, 2009. http://edition.cnn.com/2009/TECH/04/17/sweden.piracy.jail/index.html

p. 63, "one of the world's largest . . . ": "Keeping Pirates at Bay," *Economist*, September 3, 2009. www.economist.com/sciencetechnology/tq/displaystory.cfm?story_id=14299558.

p. 63, "They were sentenced to . . . ": Eric Pfanner, "Four Convicted in Sweden in Internet Piracy Case," *New York Times*, April 18, 2009.

p. 63, "bizarre . . . We can't pay . . . ": British Broadcasting Corporation, "Court jails Pirate Bay founders,." *BBC News*, April 17, 2009, http://news.bbc.co.uk/2/hi/8003799.stm.

p. 63, "The Swedish Pirate Party won . . . ": Clay Risen, "Ahoy, Germany!" *Newsweek*, September 24, 2009. www.newsweek.com/id/216108.

p. 64, "Today's results show that . . . ": International Federation of the Phonographic Industry, "Recording industry shows first results of international campaign against illegal file sharing," IFPI, London, June 8, 2004, www.ifpi.org/content/section_news/20040608.html.

p. 67, "necessary to protect . . . ": *Jurist*, "China's WTO appeal on US media imports is one of many recent worldwide protectionist measures," http://jurist.law.pitt.edu/hotline/2009_09_01_indexarch.php.

p. 69, "by committing mass copyright . . . ": International Federation of the Phonographic Industry, "Recording Industry steps up campaign against internet piracy in China," IFPI, Beijing, February 4, 2008 www.ifpi.org/content/section_news/20080204.html.

p. 70, "The music industry in China wants . . . ": International Federation of the Phonographic Industry, "Recording Industry steps up campaign against internet piracy in China,"www.ifpi.org/content/section_news/20080204.html.

p. 70, ". . . piracy was responsible for 99 percent . . . ": Kate Holton, Reuters, "China vows to crack down on Internet piracy," Reuters online news service,January 27, 2008, www.reuters.com/article/internetNews/idUSL2716617820080127.

p. 70, "I am not sure of the accuracy of . . . ": Holton, "China vows to crack down," www.reuters.com/article/internetNews/idUS L2716617820080127.

p. 70, "On the Isle of Man . . . ": Nate Anderson, "Isle of Man gets unlimited music downloads with blanket fee," *Ars Technica*, January 19, 2009, http://arstechnica.com/media/news/2009/01/isle-of-man-gets-unlimited-music-downloads-with-blanket-fee.ars.

p. 70, "What, are we going to say . . . ": Andrea Tzortzis, "People's Television," *Newsweek*, December 13, 2004.

p. 70–71, "PCF is a founder of . . . ": Participatory Culture Foundation, "Open Video Alliance," http://www.participatoryculture.org/.

p. 72, "Open-source, non-profit video player . . . ": Participatory Culture Foundation, www.participatoryculture.org.

p. 72, "The bottom line is you are going . . . ": Michael Seaver.

"Across Irish Sea: two bold tactics against music piracy," *Christian Science Monitor*, February 4, 2009, http://features.csmonitor.com/innovation/2009/02/04/across-irish-sea-two-bold-tactics-against-music-piracy/.

Chapter 5

p. 76, "You wouldn't take a CD . . . ": John Reinan, "Feds Take a Nip-it-in-the-bud Approach to Internet Piracy," *Star Tribune* (Minneapolis, MN), September 13, 2006.

p. 76, "you-name-it": Nicholas Carlson, "You Name the Price for Next Radiohead Album," *internetnews.com*, October 2, 2007, www.internetnews.com/bus-news/article.php/3702911.

p. 76, " . . . seen as a direct response to . . . ": Juliette Garside, "Radiohead generation believes music is free," *telegraph.co.uk*, October 7, 2007, http://www.telegraph.co.uk/finance/markets/2817231/Radiohead-generation-believes-music-is-free.html.

p. 77, " . . . should pay for their art . . .": "Radiohead new album: What YOU are paying for the record." *NME News*, IPC Media, October 2, 2007, www.nme.com/news/radiohead/31506.

p. 79, "Google cofounder Sergey . . .": Sergey Brin, interview by Laura Sydell, "Google's Book Scanning Has Authors On Edge," *All Things Considered*, NPR, September 2, 2009, www.npr.org/templates/transcript/transcript.php?storyId=112484311.

p. 81, "The books were a . . .": Sydell, "Google's Book Scanning Has Authors On Edge," September 2, 2009.

All websites available and accessible as of April 23, 2010.

Further Information

Books

Bingham, Jane. *Internet Freedom: Where Is the Limit?* Chicago: Heinemann Library, 2007.

Fisher III, William W. *Promises to Keep: Technology, Law, and the Future of Entertainment.* Stanford, CA: Stanford University Press, 2004.

Shepard, Heather L., and Matthew Lance Cole. *The Complete Guide to Patents, Copyrights, and Trademarks: What You Need to Know Explained Simply.* Ocala, FL: Atlantic Publishing Company, 2008.

Torr, James D., ed. *Internet Piracy.* New York: Gale Cengage Learning, 2005.

Organizations

Business Software Alliance (BSA)

www.bsa.org/country.aspx?sc_lang=en

From BSA: "The Business Software Alliance (BSA) is the voice of the world's software industry and its hardware partners on a wide range of business and policy affairs. BSA's mission is to promote conditions in which the information technology (IT) industry can thrive and contribute to the prosperity, security, and quality of life of all people.

"BSA is the largest and most international IT industry group, with policy, legal and/or educational programs in 80 countries. While several of BSA's initiatives are global in scope, most of its policy, legal, and educational efforts are led and conducted at the national level, with a growing emphasis on emerging economies."

Directors Guild of America (DGA)

www.dga.org

From DGA: "through the collective voices of more than 14,000 members that the DGA represents, the Guild seeks to protect directorial teams' legal and artistic rights, contend for their creative freedom, and strengthen their ability to develop meaningful and credible careers."

Electronic Frontier Foundation (EFF)

www.eff.org

From EFF: "EFF is . . . a civil liberties group defending your rights in the digital world."

First Amendment Center

www.firstamendmentcenter.org

From First Amendment Center: "The First Amendment Center Online offers one-stop access to information about the First Amendment. Useful for journalists, lawyers, policy makers, educators and the public . . ." This website offers research information, daily news, analysis, commentary, overviews, trends, and case law about First Amendment topics.

Intellectual Property Watch (IP-Watch)

www.ip-watch.org

From IP-Watch: "*Intellectual Property Watch*, a non-profit independent news service, reports on the interests and behind-the-scenes dynamics that influence the design and implementation of international intellectual property policies."

International Federation of the Phonographic Industry (IFPI)

www.ifpi.org

From IFPI: "IFPI's Mission: Promote the value of recorded music; Safeguard the rights of record producers; Expand the commercial uses of recorded music."

Motion Picture Association of America (MPAA)

www.mpaa.org

From MPAA: "The Motion Picture Association of America (MPAA) and its international counterpart, the Motion Picture Association (MPA) serve as the voice and advocate of the American motion picture, home video and television industries, domestically through the MPAA and internationally through the MPA."

Recording Industry of America (RIAA)

www.riaa.com

From RIAA: "The Recording Industry Association of America (RIAA) is the trade group that represents the U.S. recording industry. Its mission is to foster a business and legal climate that supports and promotes our members' creative and financial vitality. Its members are the record companies that comprise the most vibrant national music industry in the world. RIAA members create, manufacture and/or distribute approximately 85% of all legitimate sound recordings produced and sold in the United States."

Public Knowledge

www.publicknowledge.org

From Public Knowledge: "Public Knowledge is a Washington, DC based public interest group working to defend your rights in the emerging digital culture."

United States Copyright Office

www.copyright.gov

From U.S. Copyright Office: "To promote the progress of science and useful arts, by securing for limited times to authors and inventors the exclusive right to their respective writings and discoveries" (U.S. Constitution, Article I, Section 8).

World Intellectual Property Organization (WIPO)

www.wipo.int/portal/index.html.en

From WIPO: "The World Intellectual Property Organization (WIPO) is a specialized agency of the United Nations. It is dedicated to developing a balanced and accessible international intellectual property (IP) system, which rewards creativity, stimulates innovation and contributes to economic development while safeguarding the public interest."

Bibliography

Books

Clifford, Ralph D., ed. *Cybercrime: The Investigation, Prosecution and Defense of a Computer-Related Crime.* Durham, North Carolina: Carolina Academic Press, 2006.

McQuade, Sam C. *Understanding and Managing Cybercrime.* Boston: Allyn & Bacon, 2005.

Spence, Michael. *Intellectual Property.* New York: Oxford University Press, 2007.

Websites

Anderson, Nate. "Isle of Man Gets Unlimited Music Downloads with Blanket Fee." *Ars Technica,* January 19, 2009. http://arstech nica.com/media/news/2009/01/isle-of-man-gets-unlimited-music-downloads-with-blanket-fee.ars.

———. "RIAA Graduated Response Plan: Q & A with Cary Sherman." *Ars Technica,* December 21, 2008. http://arstechnica.com/old/content/2008/12/riaa-graduated-response-plan-qa-with-cary-sherman.ars.

Barrett, Sheridan, and Kurt Soller. "The Web Masters." *Newsweek*, December 22, 2008. www.newsweek.com/id/176664.

Borland, John. "RIAA Sues Campus File-Swappers." *CNET News*, April 3, 2003. http://news.cnet.com/2100-1027-995429.html.

———. "Unreleased Madonna Single Slips onto Net." *CNET News*, CNET. June 1, 2005. http://news.cnet.com/2100-1023-241 341.html.

Braiker, Brian. "Viral Video." *Newsweek*, June 15, 2007. www.news week.com/id/33938.

Brinn, Sergey. "Google's Book Scanning Has Authors on Edge." Interview by Laura Sydell, *All Things Considered*. PBS. September 2, 2009. http://www.npr.org/templates/transcript/transcript.php? storyId=112484311.

BBC News. "Court Jails Pirate Bay Founders." British Broadcasting Corporation. April 17, 2009. http://news.bbc.co.uk/2/ hi/8003799.stm.

Bruno, Anthony. "Billboard.biz Q&A: Former RIAA CEO Rosen Talks Napster." *billboardbiz.com*, June 1, 2009. www.billboard.biz/ bbbiz/search/article_display.jsp?vnu_content_id=1003978498.

Businesswire.com, "Rosetta Stone Commends Law Enforcement for Seven Piracy Arrests." *Business Wire*, October 19, 2009. www. businesswire.com/portal/site/google/?ndmViewId=news_view&ne wsId=20091019005836&newsLang=en.

Carlson, Nicholas. *internetnews.com*, October 2, 2007. www. internetnews.com/bus-news/article.php/3702911.

Cnn.com. "Four Found Guilty in Landmark Pirate Bay Case." Cable News Network. http://edition.cnn.com/2009/TECH/04/17/sweden.piracy.jail/index.html.

Curry, Neil and Mairi Mackay. "Verdict Due in Major Internet Piracy Case." *CNN.com*, April 17, 2009. www.cnn.com/2009/TECH/04/16/sweden.piracy/index.html.

DeFalco, Beth. "Teen Convicted Under Internet Piracy Law." *USA Today*, March 7, 2005. www.usatoday.com/tech/news/techpolicy/2005-03-07-az-teen-downloader-convicted_x.htm.

Economist. "Keeping Pirates at Bay." September 3, 2009. www.economist.com/sciencetechnology/tq/displaystory.cfm?story_id=14299558.

Ehert, Christian. "France Senate Approves New Version of Internet Piracy Bill." *Jurist Legal News and Research*, July 9, 2009. http://jurist.law.pitt.edu/paperchase/2009/07/france-senate-approves-new-version-of.php

Field, Kelly. "In Congress, Key Debates Lie Ahead on Costs, Accreditation, and Piracy." *The Chronicle of Higher Education*, January 11, 2008. http://chronicle.com/article/In-Congress-Key-Debates-Lie/11575/.

Gain, Bruce. "Special Report: The Future of File Sharing." May 28, 2009. www.ip-watch.org/weblog/2009/05/28/the-future-of-file sharing.

Harper, Liz. "Copyrighting in the Digital Age." *Online NewsHour* PBS, January 14, 2010. www.pbs.org/newshour/media/digital_copyright/cases.html.

Garside, Juliette. "Radiohead Generation Believes Music is Free." telegraph.co.uk, October 7, 2007. www.telegraph.co.uk/finance/markets/2817231/Radiohead-generation-believes-music-is-free.html.

Reuters. "China Vows to Crack Down on Internet Piracy." January 27, 2008. www.reuters.com/article/internetNews/idUS L2716617820080127.

Ian, Janis. "FALLOUT: A Follow Up to the Internet Debate." *janisian.com*, August 1, 2002. www.janisian.com/articles-perfsong/Fallout%20-%20rev%2011-23-05.pdf.

————. "The Internet Debacle: An Alternative View." *Performing Songwriter Magazine*, May 2009. www.janisian.com/articles-perf song/internetdebacle.pdf.

International Federation of the Phonographic Industry (IFPI) – News. "Recording Industry Steps Up Campaign Against Internet Piracy in China." February 4, 2008. www.ifpi.org/content/section _news/20080204.html.

Jackson, Brian. "France Constitutional Court Approves Internet Piracy Law." *Jurist Legal News and Research*, October 23, 2009. http://jurist.law.pitt.edu/paperchase/2009/10/france-constitutional -court-approves.php.

Marinero, Ximena. "France Lower House Approves New Version of Internet Piracy Bill." *Jurist Legal News and Research*, September 16, 2009. http://jurist.law.pitt.edu/paperchase/2009/09/france-lower-house-approves-new-version.php.

Matyszczyk, Chris. "Shakira Says File Sharing is Just Fine," *CNET*

News, October 21, 2009. http://news.cnet.com/8301-17852_3-10380995-71.html.

McCurry, Mike, and Mark McKinnon. "Getting to Yes." Billboard. biz, May 9, 2009. www.billboard.biz/bbbiz/search/article_display. jsp?vnu_content_id=1003968344&imw=Y.

McNutt, Chelsea. "The Problem of Internet Piracy Gains Attention." *VOANews,* August 28, 2007.www.voanews.com/english/archive/2007-08/2007-08-28-voa21.cfm?moddate=2007-08-28.

"MGM v. Grokster." Electronic Frontier Foundation, March 25, 2009. http://w2.eff.org/IP/P2P/MGM_v_Grokster.

Motion Picture Association of America (MPAA). "State Law." June 5, 2009. www.mapp.org/piracy_StateLaw.asp.

Murph, Darren. "Best Buy Acquires Napster for $121 Million." *endgadget.com,* September 15, 2008. www.engadget.com/2008/09/15/best-buy-acquires-napster-for-121-million.

Newsweek. "Can Buy Me Love," January 7, 2003. www.newsweek.com/id/62532.

Norton, William K. "Internet & First Amendment: Copyright, P2P & Google." First Amendment Center, June 10, 2009. www.firstamendmentcenter.org/speech/internet/topic.aspx?topic=file_sharing.

Paine, Andre. "Elton John Joins File sharing Debate." Billboard. biz. www.billboard.biz/bbbiz/content_display/industry/e3i7c69fb 437bbee15e5cdc93a07a7d2b99.

Palm, Erik. "Biggest-Ever Internet Piracy Bust Claimed in Sweden." *CNET News*, March 6, 2009. http://news.cnet.com/8301-1023_3-10190977-93.html.

Phillips, Leigh. "France Passes Tough Internet Piracy Bill." *BusinessWeek*, September 17, 2009. www.businessweek.com/globalbiz/content/sep2009/gb20090917_225687.htm.

Pike, George H. "Pay Attention to State Legislation." *Information Today*, June 2003. http://www.infotoday.com/it/jul03/index.shtml.

PublicKnowledge. "A Brief Analysis of the 'Super DMCA' Draft Model Communications Security Act." Public Knowledge, 2009. www.publicknowledge.org/reading-room/documents/policy/super-dmca-analysis.html.

Recording Industry Association of America (RIAA). "Statement of Hilary Rosen, President and CEO of the RIAA on the Napster Ruling," press release, February 12, 2001. www.riaa.com/news-item.php?news_month_filter=2&news_year_filter=2001&resultpage=2&id=F0AA1D42-E4DC-EB40-7CD5-4442CC06B345.

Risen, Clay. "Ahoy, Germany!" *Newsweek*, September 24, 2009. www.newsweek.com/id/216108.

Sandoval, Greg. "Court Orders Jammie Thomas to Pay $192 Million." cnet news, June 18, 2009. http://news.cnet.com/8301-1023-_3-10268199-93.html.

Taylor, Adam. "Europe Stumbling in Efforts to Battle Internet Piracy." *Time* in Partnership with CNN, June 13, 2009. www.time.com/time/business/article/0,8599,1904425,00.html.

Thompson, Jason. "Copyright on Trial." *StreamingMedia.com*, May 30, 2001. http://www.streamingmedia.com/article.asp?id=7450.

von Lohmann, Fred. "State 'Super-DMCA' Legislation: MPAA's Stealth Attack on Your Living Room." Electronic Frontier Foundation, March 10, 2009. http://w2.eff.org/IP/DMCA/states/200304_sdmca_eff_analysis.php.

All websites available and accessible as of April 23, 2010.

Magazines

Bennett, Ray and Joel Taylor. "IFPI Study Says Crackdown Curtailing Internet Piracy." *Hollywood Reporter*, June 15–21, 2004.

Economist. "The Spider and the Web."August 27, 2009.

Galuszka, Peter. "The War over Internet Piracy." *Black Issues in Higher Education*, March 11, 2004.

Grant, Daniel. "Internet Piracy of Copyrighted Art." *American Artist*, August 2004.

Greenberg, James and William Triplett. "Internet Theft: How It Happens and Why It Matters." *DGA Quarterly*, Fall 2009.

Holland, Bill. "RIAA Sues Individuals Over Copyright." *Billboard*, April 12, 2003.

Levy, Steven. "The Noisy War Over Napster." *Newsweek*, June 5, 2000.

———. "Rip This Book? Not Yet." *Newsweek*, February 18, 2008.

———. "A Very Dangerous Supremes Rerun." *Newsweek*, April 4, 2005.

McClure, Dave. "Copyright Wars 2001: Will ISPs survive:?" *Boardwatch*, October 2000.

Newsweek. "Napster's Autopsy." April 21, 2003.

———. "A Piracy Culture." January 16, 2006.

Tzortzis, Andrea. "People's Television." *Newsweek*, December 13, 2004.

Underhill, William. "Music for Free, and It's Legal." *Newsweek*, March 30, 2009.

Whitney, Daisy. "As Piracy Climbs, TV Takes Up Arms." *TV Week*, May 18, 2009.

Newspapers

Duhigg, Charles, Chris Gaither, and Dawn C. Chmielewski. *Los Angeles Times*, September 28, 2006, Home ed.

Martin, Mark and Lynda Gledhill. "Governor Signs Internet Piracy Bill." *San Francisco Chronicle*, September 22, 2004, Final ed.

McCaffrey, Shannon. "U. S. Targets Internet Piracy Groups." *Philadelphia Inquirer*, July 1, 2005.

Nowlin, Sanford. "AT&T Slammed Over Piracy Plan." *San Antonio Express-News*, June 15, 2007, State and Metro ed.

Oakes, Larry. "Brainerd Mom Takes On Music Industry." *Star Tribune* (Minneapolis, MN), October 3, 2007.

Patrick, Aaron O., and Sarah McBride. "Showdown Looms Over Pirated-Media Directory: Swedish Prosecutors Target Organizers of Pirate Bay, A Huge File sharing Guide." *Wall Street Journal*, January 11, 2008. Eastern ed.

Pfanner, Eric. "Four Convicted in Sweden in Internet Piracy Case." *New York Times*, April 18, 2009. Late ed. (East Coast).

———. "France Approves Crackdown on Internet Piracy." *New York Times*, May 13, 2009.

———. "Isle of Man Piracy Suits Target College Network Users." *Los Angeles Times*, May 1, 2005.

Reinan, John. "Feds Take a Nip-it-in-the-bud Approach to Internet Piracy." *Star Tribune* (Minneapolis, MN), September 13, 2006, Metro ed.

Sherman, Mark. "Government Launches Internet Piracy Offensive." *Washington Post*, July 1, 2005, Final ed.

Wall Street Journal. "Fighting Internet Piracy—Plan B." May 15, 2006, Eastern ed.

Wood, Sam. "Former Drexel student gets probation in Internet piracy." *Philadelphia Inquirer*, September 17, 2008.

U.S. Federal News Service

U.S. Department of Justice. *Defendant Sentenced to One Year in Federal Prison as Part of Internet Piracy Crackdown.* (Western District of North Carolina, November 1, 2007). www.justice.gov/criminal/cybercrime/yaghmaiSent.htm.

U.S. Department of Justice. *Defendant Sentenced to One Year and One Day in Federal Prison as Part of Internet Piracy Crackdown.* (U.S. Attorney's Office for the Western District of North Carolina, April 24, 2007). www.justice.gov/usao/ncw/press/fastlink.html.

U.S. Department of Justice. *Federal Law Enforcement Targets International Internet Piracy Syndicates.* (Washington, DC, December 11, 2001). www.justice.gov/opa/pr/2001/December/01_crm_643.htm.

U.S. Federal News Service. *BSA Raises the Stakes in the Fight Against Software Piracy Online Extends $1 Million Reward to Qualified Reports of Internet Piracy.* (Washington, DC, April 3, 2008).

U.S. Federal News Service. *Higher Education, Entertainment Industry Witnesses Detail Impact of Efforts to Combat Internet Piracy on College Campuses.* (Washington, DC, September 26, 2006).

U.S. Department of Justice. *Justice Department Announces International Internet Piracy Sweep.* (Washington, DC, April 22, 2004). www.justice.gov/archive/opa/pr/2005/June/05_crm_353.htm.

U. S. Department of Justice. *Man Pleads Guilty to Internet piracy of Star Wars Film.* (Northern District of California, December 15, 2000). www.justice.gov/criminal/cybercrime/spataforeplea.htm.

Court Decisions

MGM et al. v. *Grokster, Ltd., et al.*, 545 U. S. 913 (2005)

RIAA v. *Napster, Inc.*, No. C 99-05183 MHP, 2000 WL 573136 (2001)

RIAA v. *Napster, Inc.*, 239 F.3d 1004 (9th Cir. 2001)

RIAA v. *Verizon Internet Services, Inc.*, 351 F.3d 1229 (D.C. Cir. 2003)

Sony Corp. of America v. *Universal City Studios, Inc.*, 464 U.S. 417 (1984)

Legislation

Digital Theft Deterrence and Copyright Damages Improvement Act of 1999

The Digital Millennium Copyright Act of 1998

Family Entertainment and Copyright Act of 2005

The No Electronic Theft (NET) Act

Journals and Studies

Band, Jonathan. "The Copyright Paradox." *The Brookings Review* (Winter 2001).

Business Software Alliance. "Faces of Internet Piracy."http://global. bsa.org/faces/index.html.

———. "Sixth Annual BSA-IDC Global Software '08 Piracy Study." http://global.bsa.org/globalpiracy2008/index.html.

Herings, P. Jean-Jacques, Ronald Peters, and Michael S. Yang. "Piracy on the Internet: Accommodate It or Fight It?" *Meteor* (2009): 1-26.

Hinduja, Sameer. "Correlates of Internet Software Piracy." *Journal of Contemporary Justice*, 17.4 (2001):

Index

Page numbers in **boldface** are illustrations, tables, and charts.

About the Author

GAIL BLASSER RILEY is the award-winning author of more than four hundred books, articles, and educational pieces for children and adults. She is a former prosecutor and business law professor. Riley is fluent in French and conversant in Spanish; these skills are immensely valuable as she utilizes reference resources from a variety of countries. Riley's books, on topics such as the Supreme Court *Miranda* ruling and censorship, have garnered honors from the Children's Book Council, New York Public Library, and Young Adult Library Services Association. This is her first book for Marshall Cavendish Benchmark.